✧ *Companions for the Journey* ✧

Praying with Dominic

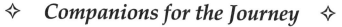

✧ Companions for the Journey ✧

Praying with Dominic

by
Michael Monshau, OP

Saint Mary's Press
Christian Brothers Publications
Winona, Minnesota

To
✧ my brothers, ✧
the friars of
the Chicago Dominican Province

The publishing team for this book included Carl Koch, FSC, development editor; Amy Schlumpf Manion, manuscript editor and typesetter; Elaine Kohner, illustrator; pre-press, printing, and binding by the graphics division of Saint Mary's Press.

The psalms in this book are from *Psalms Anew: In Inclusive Language*, compiled by Nancy Schreck and Maureen Leach (Winona, MN: Saint Mary's Press, 1986). Copyright © 1986 by Saint Mary's Press. All rights reserved.

The scriptural material found on pages 30–31 and 63 is freely adapted to make it inclusive regarding gender. These adaptations are not to be understood or used as official translations of the Bible.

All other scriptural quotations used in this book are from the New Jerusalem Bible. Copyright © 1985 by Darton, Longman & Todd, London; and Doubleday, a division of Bantam, Doubleday, Dell Publishing Group, New York. Used with permission.

The acknowledgments continue on page 118.

Printed in the United States of America

Printing: 6 5 4 3 2 1

Year: 1999 98 97 96 95 94 93

ISBN 0-88489-288-3

✧ Contents ✧

Foreword   7

Preface   13

Introduction   15

Meditations

1. **Preaching**   *28*

2. **Sacred Study**   *35*

3. **Putting on the Truth**   *41*

4. **To Praise, to Bless**   *47*

5. **Movement as Adoration**   *54*

6. **Prayerful Journeys**   *60*

7. **Liturgy, the Community at Prayer**   *65*

8. **Christ Crucified**   *71*

9. **Mary, Model of Discipleship**   *76*

10. **Trust**   *84*

11. **Humility**   *90*

12. **Freedom**   *96*

13. **Mercy and Compassion**   *102*

14. **Charity**   *107*

15. **Perseverance**   *112*

For Further Reading   *117*

✧ Foreword ✧

Companions for the Journey

Just as food is required for human life, so are companions. Indeed, the word *companions* comes from two Latin words: *com*, meaning "with," and *panis*, meaning "bread." Companions nourish our heart, mind, soul, and body. They are also the people with whom we can celebrate the sharing of bread.

Perhaps the most touching stories in the Bible are about companionship: the Last Supper, the wedding feast at Cana, the sharing of the loaves and the fishes, and Jesus' breaking of bread with the disciples on the road to Emmaus. Each incident of companionship with Jesus revealed more about his mercy, love, wisdom, suffering, and hope. When Jesus went to pray in the Garden of Olives, he craved the companionship of the Apostles. They let him down. But God sent the Spirit to inflame the hearts of the Apostles, and they became faithful companions to Jesus and to each other.

Throughout history, other faithful companions have followed Jesus and the Apostles. These saints and mystics have also taken the journey from conversion, through suffering, to resurrection. Just as they were inspired by the holy people who went before them, so too may you take them as your companions as you walk on your spiritual journey.

The Companions for the Journey series is a response to the spiritual hunger of Christians. This series makes available the rich spiritual teachings of mystics and guides whose wisdom can help us on our pilgrimages. As you complete the last meditation in each volume, it is hoped that you will feel supported, challenged, and affirmed by a soul-companion on your spiritual journey.

The spiritual hunger that has emerged over the last twenty years is a great sign of renewal in Christian life. People fill retreat programs and workshops on topics in spirituality. The demand for spiritual directors exceeds the number available. Interest in the lives and writings of saints and mystics is increasing as people search for models of whole and holy Christian life.

Praying with Dominic

Praying with Dominic is more than just a book about Dominic's spirituality. This book seeks to engage you in praying in the way that Dominic did about issues and themes that were central to his experience. Each meditation can enlighten your understanding of his spirituality and lead you to reflect on your own experience.

The goal of *Praying with Dominic* is that you will discover Dominic's rich spirituality and integrate his spirit and wisdom into your relationship with God, with your brothers and sisters, and with your own heart and mind.

Suggestions for Praying with Dominic

Meet Dominic, a fascinating companion for your pilgrimage, by reading the introduction to this book, which begins on page 15. It provides a brief biography of Dominic and an outline of the major themes of his spirituality.

Once you meet Dominic, you will be ready to pray with him and to encounter God, your sisters and brothers, and yourself in new and wonderful ways. To help your prayer, here are some suggestions that have been part of the tradition of Christian spirituality:

Create a sacred space. Jesus said, "When you pray, go to your private room, shut yourself in, and so pray to your [God] who is in that secret place, and your [God] who sees all that is done in secret will reward you'" (Matthew 6:6). Solitary prayer is best done in a place where you can have privacy and silence, both of which can be luxuries in the life of busy people.

If privacy and silence are not possible, create a quiet, safe place within yourself, perhaps while riding to and from work, while sitting in line at the dentist's office, or while waiting for someone. Do the best you can, knowing that a loving God is present everywhere. Whether the meditations in this book are used for solitary prayer or with a group, try to create a prayerful mood with candles, meditative music, an open Bible, or a crucifix.

Open yourself to the power of prayer. Every human experience has a religious dimension. All of life is suffused with God's presence. So remind yourself that God is present as you begin your period of prayer. Do not worry about distractions. If something keeps intruding during your prayer, spend some time talking with God about it. Be flexible because God's Spirit blows where it will.

Prayer can open your mind and widen your vision. Be open to new ways of seeing God, people, and yourself. As you open yourself to the Spirit of God, different emotions are evoked, such as sadness from tender memories, or joy from a celebration recalled. Our emotions are messages from God that can tell us much about our spiritual quest. Also, prayer strengthens our will to act. Through prayer, God can touch our will and empower us to live according to what we know is true.

Finally, many of the meditations in this book will call you to employ your memories, your imagination, and the circumstances of your life as subjects for prayer. The great mystics and saints realized that they had to use all their resources to know God better. Indeed, God speaks to us continually and touches us constantly. We must learn to listen and feel with all the means that God has given us.

Come to prayer with an open mind, heart, and will.

Preview each meditation before beginning. After you have placed yourself in God's presence, spend a few moments previewing the readings and especially the reflection activities. Several reflection activities are given in each meditation because different styles of prayer appeal to different personalities or personal needs. **Note that each meditation has more**

reflection activities than can be done during one prayer period. Therefore, select only one or two reflection activities each time you use a meditation. Do not feel compelled to complete all the reflection activities.

Read meditatively. Each meditation offers you a story about Dominic and a reading based on his words. Take your time reading. If a particular phrase touches you, stay with it. Relish its feelings, meanings, and concerns.

Use the reflections. Following the readings is a short reflection in commentary form, which is meant to give perspective to the readings. Then you are offered several ways of meditating on the readings and the theme of the prayer. You may be familiar with the different methods of meditating, but in case you are not, they are described briefly here:

✦ *Repeated short prayer or mantra:* One means of focusing your prayer is to use a *mantra,* or "prayer word." The mantra may be a single word or a short phrase taken from the readings or from the Scriptures. For example, in the reflection activities in meditation 5 in this book, a short prayer is simply the name of Jesus. Repeated slowly in harmony with your breathing, the mantra helps you center your heart and mind on one action or attribute of God.

✦ *Lectio divina:* This type of meditation is "divine studying," a concentrated reflection on the word of God or the wisdom of a spiritual writer. Most often in *lectio divina,* you will be invited to read one of the passages several times and then concentrate on one or two sentences, pondering their meaning for you and their effect on you. *Lectio divina* commonly ends with formulation of a resolution.

✦ *Guided meditation:* In this type of meditation, our imagination helps us consider alternative actions and likely consequences. Our imagination helps us experience new ways of seeing God, our neighbors, ourselves, and nature. When Jesus told his followers parables and stories, he engaged their imagination. In this book, you will be invited to follow guided meditations.

One way of doing a guided meditation is to read the scene or story several times, until you know the outline and can recall it when you enter into reflection. Or before your prayer time, you may wish to record the meditation on a tape recorder. If so, remember to allow pauses for reflection between phrases and to speak with a slow, peaceful pace and tone. Then, during prayer, when you have finished the readings and the reflection commentary, you can turn on your recording of the meditation and be led through it. If you find your own voice too distracting, ask a friend to make the tape for you.

✦ *Examen of consciousness:* The reflections often will ask you to examine how God has been speaking to you in your past and present experience—in other words, the reflections will ask you to examine your awareness of God's presence in your life.

✦ *Journal writing:* Writing is a process of discovery. If you write for any length of time, stating honestly what is on your mind and in your heart, you will unearth much about who you are, how you stand with your God, what deep longings reside in your soul, and more. In some reflections, you will be asked to write a dialog with Jesus or someone else. If you have never used writing as a means of meditation, try it. Reserve a special notebook for your journal writing. If desired, you can go back to your entries at a future time for an examen of consciousness.

✦ *Action:* Occasionally, a reflection will suggest singing a favorite hymn, going out for a walk, or undertaking some other physical activity. Actions can be meaningful forms of prayer.

Using the Meditations for Group Prayer

If you wish to use the meditations for community prayer, these suggestions may help:

✦ Read the theme to the group. Call the community into the presence of God, using the short opening prayer. Invite one or two participants to read one or both readings. If you use both readings, observe the pause between them.

✦ The reflection commentary may be used as a reading, or it can be deleted, depending on the needs and interests of the group.

✦ Select one of the reflection activities for your group. Allow sufficient time for your group to reflect, to recite a centering prayer or mantra, to accomplish a studying prayer (*lectio divina*), or to finish an examen of consciousness. Depending on the group and the amount of available time, you may want to invite the participants to share their reflections, responses, or petitions with the group.

✦ Reading the passage from the Scriptures may serve as a summary of the meditation.

✦ If a formulated prayer or a psalm is given as a closing, it may be recited by the entire group. Or you may ask participants to offer their own prayers for the closing.

Now you are ready to begin praying with Dominic, a faithful and caring companion on this stage of your spiritual journey. It is hoped that you will find him to be a true soul-companion.

CARL KOCH, FSC
Editor

✧ Preface ✧

The Companions for the Journey series on prayer presents a wonderful opportunity for Saint Dominic's relatively unpublicized life of prayer to be shared with others. Dominic lived in a milieu in which popular devotion quickly surrounded notable holy persons after their death. However, the earliest Dominicans seem to have discouraged the development of such devotion in his case. They were concerned that if the man himself were emphasized, his work, the Holy Preaching, would be neglected, and the Holy Preaching is clearly what Dominic's life was all about.

As a result, for the nearly eight centuries since Dominic's death, although his name and order are rather well known, very little has been written about his life and manner of prayer. This book joins other recent efforts at redressing this omission.

Many people have nurtured this project, and I am grateful to them. While writing this book, I lived among the Dominican Sisters who are in residence at the Maria Health Care Center in Adrian, Michigan. Their ceaseless encouragement and interest have certainly been an important part of this work. Also, since its inception, the contemplative Dominican nuns at Farmington Hills, Michigan, have taken this project to their hearts and prayers, and I have been sustained by their interest.

In particular I thank a trio of Dominicans whose assistance in this project has been invaluable. Edward Ruane, OP, helped with my plans for the entire outline of the meditations. Elizabeth Jenkins, OP, generously proofread the text, and Cathleen Going, OP, provided a theological critique before the final draft was submitted to the publisher.

At the publishing end of the project, I found the creative and professional input from Carl Koch, FSC, to be instructive and delightful.

Most of all, I am indebted to that group of Dominicans through whom I have come to know Dominic and his preaching mission and to whom I dedicate this book: my brothers, the friars of the Chicago Dominican Province.

✧ Introduction ✧

Who Was Dominic?

In *The Divine Comedy*, when the poet Dante wanted to criticize corruption in the church, he sang the praises of Dominic, whose only desire was to spread the Gospel by preaching and living a simple life:

> Dominic was his name, whose work and worth
> I publish, as the husbandman whom Christ
> Called to His garden to help till the earth.

> Right well the friend and messenger of Christ
> He showed him, for the first love he displayed
> Was love for the first counsel given by Christ.

> Full many a time his nurse would find him laid
> On the bare ground, silent and wide awake,
> As though to say: "For this end I was made."

> . . . .

> He grew a mighty doctor soon, who scanned
> In every part that vine which, all too sure
> Withers if dressed by an unskilful hand.

> And from that See which once, but now no more—
> (I blame not it, but him who there doth fix
> His cankered sway) cherished the righteous poor,

> No leave to pay out three or two for six,
> No tithes *quae pauperum Dei sunt* sought he,
> Nor first cut at fat stalls and bishoprics,

But only licence to fight ceaselessly
> Against the erring world for that good seed
> Whence four-and-twenty scions girdle thee.

With Apostolic sanction guaranteed,
> Equipped with doctrine and with zeal as well,
> Like some high torrent thundering down at speed

On briars and brakes of heresy he fell
> Uprooting them, and still was swift to go
> Where opposition was most formidable.

From him, unnumbered rillets took their flow
> To irrigate the Catholic garden-plot
> Thenceforth, whence all its bushes greener grow.
> (*The Divine Comedy*, bk. 3, canto 7, lines 70–105)

Indeed Dominic's influence was extensive. However, for someone this famous and powerful and for the founder of one of the great religious communities in church history—the Order of Preachers, or more familiarly, the Dominicans—amazingly little is known about Dominic. He preached constantly, but wrote almost nothing. A true mendicant, he traveled about spreading the Gospel to anyone who would listen. Had he written, few in his audience could have read his writings anyway. Later Dominicans like Albertus Magnus and Thomas Aquinas would become giants of the written word, but a fire burned in Dominic to preach. This was his charism.

Unlike his contemporary Francis of Assisi, Dominic did not inspire many legends. Myth credits him with originating the devotion to the rosary, but even this legend has little basis in records of his life. Indeed, as was common in his day, much of his story is hagiography, or an idealized biography. Many of the stories cited in this book are based on this hagiography. The events have a historical foundation, but the tone may seem pietistic to modern readers.

Whereas other great leaders left the imprint of their personality upon their followers and the church in general, Dominic bequeathed primarily his work—the Holy Preaching. The Holy Preaching was his passion, the focus on which he fashioned the supports for the spiritual life that he bequeathed to his followers. This absorbing task defined and gave vibrancy to his entire life.

Despite the scarcity of primary sources about Dominic, what we do know about him testifies to the rich spirituality capable of inspiring contemporary pilgrims, just as it inspired later Dominicans like Catherine of Siena, Bartolomé de las Casas, Rose of Lima, Martín de Porres, Meister Eckehart, Heinrich Süse, Vincent Ferrer, and others.

Dominic's Early Life

Caleruega, a village situated in the north central Spanish province of Burgos, is holy ground for the Order of Preachers—sisters, friars, nuns, laity—and their associates, because it is Dominic's birthplace.

A small, quiet community nestled on the side of a gently sloping hill in the midst of flat farmland, Caleruega bears obvious signs of Dominic's influence. The only large buildings in the village are the Dominican compound that surrounds the Guzman family home and the Tower of Caleruega, a several-story tower that belonged to the Guzman family, the royal wardens or lesser nobility of Burgos. The tower looms large in the courtyard of the priory of the Dominican friars, where a novitiate and a spirituality center are housed.

A monastery of contemplative Dominican nuns adjoins the friars' priory. The parish church stands adjacent to the priory. A monument to Dominic dominates the village center. Villagers come and go, sometimes stopping to make a short visit in either of the public chapels or the parish church or to buy pastries at the nuns' monastery. The focal point for miles around is the cross at the peak of the hill on which Caleruega is situated.

Born in 1170, Dominic was probably the third of four or five children of Jane d'Aza and Felix de Guzman. Two brothers, most likely already seminarians at the time of his birth, preceded Dominic. According to most accounts, at the age of seven, Dominic moved to the village of Gumiel de Hizán. Tradition maintains that Jane d'Aza's brother was the parish priest in this community and that Dominic studied under his priest-uncle. Biographers suggest that several characteristics emerged during this period that would mark Dominic's entire life.

Dominic seemed to prefer study to the typical games of other children. He excelled at his studies and quickly surpassed his classmates. Stories indicate that he manifested great compassion and sensitivity for people who were poor or suffering. During this time, he began ascetical practices that were then popular expressions of devotion and Christlikeness. As Dante wrote:

> Full many a time his nurse would find him laid
>> On the bare ground, silent and wide awake,
>> As though to say: "For this end I was made."
>> (*The Divine Comedy*, bk. 3, canto 7, lines 76–78)

At the age of fourteen Dominic moved again, this time to Palencia, where he commenced six years of university studies. His early courses probably were devoted to logic, grammar, and rhetoric. Later he matriculated in mathematics, science, and music. Following these six years, he began his theological studies, preparing himself for the canonry that he would eventually assume.

During the period of his studies, Dominic lived frugally, possessing little and taking the most meager food and drink. Some accounts claim that he drank no wine during this entire period. His conviction that the Gospel called him to a radical life of witness is evidenced by at least two stories about him. In one instance, Dominic attempted to sell himself into slavery in exchange for an unfortunate captive whose sorry plight had come to Dominic's attention. In another story, the experience of seeing people living in terrible poverty so moved Dominic that he sold his prized and expensive books and gave the money to feed the people. When questioned about this, Dominic responded, "'I could not bear to prize dead skins when living skins were starving and in want'" (Bede Jarrett, *Life of St Dominic, 1170–1221*, p. 11).

Dominic's Contemplative Years

At approximately the age of twenty-five, Dominic was ordained to the priesthood and began his life as a member of the canonry in the town of Osma, Spain. By Dominic's time, canons had a unique role in the church. Bishops would gather some of their priests into households, usually attached to a cathedral or a large, urban church. Canons prayed the entire Liturgy of the Hours, as monks did. Similarly, they were expected to live simply, not accumulating wealth or offices. In some locations, the canons lived communally and enclosed the way monks did, with the only obvious distinction being that monks lived in remote settings whereas canons dwelled in cities. In other places, canons accepted administrative duties for the local diocese and some degree of pastoral responsibility for the faithful. The degree to which canons undertook pastoral responsibilities varied from place to place.

Tradition holds that Dominic rarely left the cloister during his decade as a canon. Dominic's time as a canon has been described this way:

> "Straightway he began to appear among his brother canons as a bright ray of sunshine, in humbleness of heart the least, in holiness the first, shedding around him the fragrance of quickening life, like the sweet scent of pinewoods in the heat of a summer's day. And advancing from strength to strength as does the wide-growing olive and the slender, lofty cypress, day and night he frequented the Church, ceaselessly devoted to prayer, scarcely venturing beyond the cloister walls, the more to find leisure for his lone thoughts with God." (Jarrett, *Life*, p. 14)

These contemplative years left their mark on Dominic, for as busy as he would later become, he remained attentive to daily, extended sessions of prayer, sometimes lasting into and throughout the night.

Dominic the Preacher

In 1203, Diego d'Azevedo, Dominic's bishop, summoned Dominic to accompany him on a diplomatic mission to Denmark. This journey and a second one, also to Denmark, marked the end of the cloistered, contemplative chapter of Dominic's life.

During their journey, Dominic and the bishop passed through the region of France in which the Albigensian sect had firmly rooted. One of Dominic's biographers gives this description of the Albigensians' views in terms that Dominic would have understood quite well:

> Matter was evil; hence every living thing was unclean; and physical life was the supreme and only misfortune.

Matter was in itself evil, and therefore to prolong the existence of matter was evil and to reproduce matter was an even greater evil. The only real act of goodness was the getting rid of life. "In the married state, salvation is impossible," said one of the heretical prophets. Said another, "The idea of parentage is the curse of the world." Said another, "To multiply human souls is to multiply damnation." Their gospel was to decry the sanctity and meaning of marriage and to cry up the celibate life, and this not out of any appreciation of its self-immolation, but out of disgust at the sheer multiplication of existences.

Similarly, suicide was considered the choicest form of death, the most hallowed. . . . The penance and austerities of the mediæval theosophists were therefore very real, for luxury was but an added crime, and anything that lessened the vigour of the flesh was a direct incentive to a purer knowledge of God. Flesh meat very properly was forbidden, the discipline freely used, ascetic and emaciated figures were the real sacrament of this logical heresy—outward and visible signs of an inner, invisible grace; and the soul, too, was to be disciplined into an absolute isolation of spirit, away and apart from life, lost in abstraction. (Jarrett, *Life*, pp. 21–22)

On one of these trips, while staying at an inn in Toulouse, Dominic debated with the Albigensian innkeeper throughout the night, attempting to convert him back to orthodoxy. By dawn, Dominic had convinced the man. This incident provided Dominic with the initial impulse to spend his life preaching, challenging others to respond to the Gospel.

During their travels, Bishop Diego and Dominic visited Rome, where Diego tried to resign his bishopric so that he could preach the Gospel to the Tartars in the East. Instead of accepting his resignation, the pope commissioned Diego to join his efforts with those of the Cistercian monks, who were preaching against the Albigensians.

Committed to placing their preaching ministry at the service of the church, Diego and Dominic readily acquiesced to the pope's desire. Albigensianism detracted from the dignity of the human person, failed to reverence life, and had disastrous effects on medieval society. Filled with compassion for people deluded by this sect, Dominic felt certain that authentic preaching of the Christian Gospel would entice the Albigensians back to the peace and solace of the true faith.

Dominic also believed that Christian preachers would have to change their ways to be successful. The Albigensian preachers lived simply, maintained strict discipline over themselves, and, in doing so, highlighted the corruption in the church. Conversely, many of the Christian preachers traveled in luxury accompanied by an impressive entourage. As a result, common folk often questioned how such preachers could give witness to the poor Christ.

To remedy this situation, Bishop Diego and Dominic chose to live modestly, even poorly, themselves. Much to the shock and disapproval of some of the church dignitaries, Diego and Dominic went about barefoot, living off the food and small coins that they begged from common people. Such simplicity of life gave credibility and power to their preaching about Jesus, the humble servant. Dominic identified himself as Brother Dominic, the name by which he was known for the rest of his life.

Equipped with the papal commission and fortified by their own commitment to Christ and to a humble lifestyle, Diego and Dominic united their efforts with those of the Cistercians, the pope's officially designated preachers against Albigensianism in the Languedoc area of France.

The Order of Preachers

The next decade of Dominic's life was devoted to public debates with the Albigensians, and to preaching and traveling on evangelical tours. In 1206, while in Fanjeaux, in southern France, Dominic intensely experienced God's call to him. Although the details of this vision are sketchy, the encounter with God reconfirmed Dominic's zeal in preaching and his determination to form a community of people willing to challenge heretics and, as important, to instruct Catholics in their faith.

Bishop Diego and Dominic gathered a group of preachers to help in their efforts to convert the Albigensians, an effort that met with more frustration than success. Then in 1207, Diego died suddenly. Dominic's reactions to the loss of his mentor are not known, but he continued his ministry undaunted.

Dominic also inherited direction of a community of women in Prouille. Nine women who wished to separate from the Albigensians had been formed into a religious community faithful to the Catholic church. Dominic assumed the direction of the community, seeing to their domestic needs and spiritual formation. Eventually, he composed a rule of life for them. This foundation became the cradle of the Dominican order.

Meanwhile, the tensions between the Catholic legation and the Albigensians had reached a state of war. The Albigensians murdered one papal legate. What started as a religious conflict soon became entangled with French politics, and a crusade ensued. The French king threw the weight of the crown against the heretics. Fighting went on for nearly forty years, ending only with the capture of an important Albigensian fortress and the execution of about two hundred of their elite members.

Even as the Crusades got underway, Dominic's preaching band formed a community, but it was not bound by vows. As their organization stabilized, many still saw themselves as dedicated to preaching solely within their own diocese. In 1215, a young man, Peter Selhan, entered the community and brought with him the gift of a residence in Toulouse (a building that still stands). This house became the focal point for the community.

In the same year, Dominic traveled to Rome to attend the Lateran Council. While there, he requested and received church approval for the nuns' foundation. Dominic sought official church sanction for his communities because he was convinced that the preaching of the Gospel had to be done in harmony with the church. The preaching community could be most effective only if it were free of local political entanglements. In 1216, Pope Honorius III recognized the order as an approved religious community in the church. They would follow the Rule of Saint Augustine complemented by their own constitutions.

In this era, Dominic's Order of Preachers seemed to be a radical creation. According to custom, only bishops had the power to preach in the name of the church. Now Dominic led a whole band of nonbishop preachers. Although strenuous objections were raised, the pope was all too aware of the need for an order of preachers. Too many Catholics had either little or no knowledge of their faith.

Only six years of Dominic's life remained. During these years, the order grew rapidly. Even though Dominic burned with the desire to send out preachers, he typically insisted that they first prepare themselves through study. After relocating from Prouille to Toulouse, Dominic actually led the procession of brothers to class himself. His example and legislations thereafter called for a life of assiduous study. Dominicans were soon studying and teaching in Paris and other centers of learning.

Dominic's vision of the mission of the Order of Preachers reached far beyond southern France. Soon after the papal approval, Dominic sent the brothers out to Italy, to Germany, and to his native Spain. Wherever the word of God needed to be preached, Dominic wanted to send friars.

As the number of friars increased, so did the convents of contemplative nuns. At the behest of the pope, Dominic organized a community of women in Rome. Soon Dominican convents were formed in Madrid, Bologna, and other cities.

By 1218, Dominic maintained his own residence at Bologna. And, although he traveled frequently, Bologna remained his official convent until his death.

The Close of Dominic's Life

In 1221, Dominic's health began to deteriorate. In July, he returned from a trip to Venice weakened and exhausted. Because of the intense July heat, the friars at the Bologna priory moved Dominic to a monastery in the hills above the city. As death drew near, the superior of this Benedictine priory generously proposed a burial site at the monastery. But Dominic asked to be buried beneath the feet of his brethren and ordered the friars to return him to their own priory.

During his final agony, Dominic uttered his last will and testament to the community. In words that Dominicans have treasured for nearly eight centuries, Dominic said, "'These are, beloved ones, the inheritances that I leave you . . . have charity among you; hold to humility; possess voluntary poverty'" (Jarrett, *Life*, p. 166).

In the early evening of 6 August 1221, Dominic died. At the time of his death, approximately three hundred friars preached in eight different countries, and four monasteries of contemplative Dominican women carried on their ministry of prayer in three different countries.

Dominic's Spirituality

Like all great Christians, Dominic tried to live with faith, hope, and love. His commitment to the Gospel was unassailable. In other words, with God's grace, he put on Jesus Christ. Nevertheless, because God respects the uniqueness of each person, Dominic's spirituality assumed certain distinct characteristics.

Holistic Prayer

Dominic's spirituality recognized the value that the various dimensions of a person's life bring to prayer. His own prayer involved his entire body, his intellect, his emotions, and his spirit. Dominic did not insist that any one form of prayer was best for all persons or that any one prayer form was the best prayer form for a single individual at all times. Dominic believed that each of us has a unique method of joining body and spirit in praise of God.

Although Dominic did not author a treatise on prayer, within the first century after his death his followers assembled a commentary called "The Nine Ways of Prayer," comprising the following:

1. bowing before the altar as if Christ were really and personally present
2. beseeching God's mercy while lying prostrate
3. performing acts of penance
4. genuflecting frequently before a crucifix

5. accompanying prayer with hand gestures and bodily movement
6. posturing oneself in the form of a cross
7. arching the entire body heavenward
8. studying Divine truth
9. praising God while traveling

The Nine Ways of Prayer were intended to assure his followers that prayer can indeed take many forms.

For Dominic, prayer was as habitual as breathing the cool
mountain air. Dominic prayed when traveling, before preaching, throughout the night, during the day, with others, and
alone.

Putting on the Truth of Christ

The passion of Dominic's life was living the Truth. The Truth
is Christ Jesus. For Dominic, life was politically and religious-
ly dysfunctional when the Truth contained in the Gospels was
obscured in any way. Thus, he persistently prayed and studied
the Scriptures and theology seeking to encounter the Truth
that is Christ. Then Dominic tried to live in ways consistent
with the Truth that he had encountered in study. Dominic acknowledged that unless the friars and he deeply knew Jesus—
the Truth—and lived in the light of this Truth, they could not
convey this Truth to other people.

Encountering the Word of God

Dominic's life was one of constant praise and blessing of God,
and of ceaseless reflection on God's word, particularly as it is
recorded in the Gospel of Matthew and the epistles of Paul.
Rooted in the Living Word, Dominic's contemplative moments were immersed in the presence and wisdom of the Holy
One. His encounter with God, through the word, fed his soul
and directed his interaction with other people.

Journeying with this faith-filled preacher reveals a pattern of careful attentiveness to the word of God, that Living
Word that is broken open and celebrated through the liturgical life of the church. The liturgy and the word of God nourished and directed Dominic's contemplation daily.

To Praise, to Bless, to Preach

Nourished by prayer, meditation, and study of the Gospels, Dominic's preaching caught fire. In fact, a motto for the order became "To praise, to bless, to preach." Dominic took Jesus' directions to the disciples in Luke's Gospel to heart and committed himself body, mind, and spirit to these words:

> "The harvest is rich, but the labourers are few, so ask the [God] of the harvest to send labourers to do [the] harvesting. . . . Whenever you go into a town where they make you welcome, eat what is put before you. Cure those in it who are sick, and say, 'The [Reign] of God is very near to you.'" (10:2–9)

Dominic understood from the core of his being that in order to believe in the Truth—Jesus Christ—people first had to hear the word of God.

Trust in Providence and Human Goodness

The way in which Dominic adapted the Rule of Saint Augustine testified to Dominic's trust in his followers. Most rules for religious mandate almost all facets of their schedule and ministry—indeed, their whole manner of living. Most founders believed that breaking the rule of the order was sinful. Dominic did not believe this.

Dominic wanted his friars and the nuns to be obedient to and commit themselves to God. Doing the will of God and performing the ministry of preaching might require dispensing themselves from specific guidelines of the rule. Dominic trusted that God's providence would lead the friars and nuns to do what was right and just.

Dominic's Influence Today

Dominic, the simple brother, the teacher of the faith, the preacher of the Gospel, and the person of prayer, drew many of his contemporaries away from confusion and led them toward Christ. In the same way, Dominic can be a faithful companion on the journey of today's Christian.

✧ **Meditation 1** ✧

Preaching

Theme: Jesus called all baptized Christians to preach the Good News. However, the manner of preaching may vary with each person. Dominic made proclaiming God's word the focus of all his energies and the center of his spirituality.

Opening prayer: Caring God, nourish me every day with your Living Word. With every thought, conversation, deed, and activity of this day, help me to give witness to that Living Word, for I know that every moment carries with it the invitation to do so.

About Dominic

During Dominic's lifetime, the Christian faith was being menaced by the rapidly growing Albigensian sect. The Albigensians denied the incarnation of Christ and held that anything material was evil. Therefore, they condemned, among other things, marriage and the consumption of most nourishing foods. They even promoted suicide by gradual starvation as a penitential practice. Dominic's earliest followers gave this account of what was probably his first face-to-face encounter with an Albigensian:

> Diego d'Acabes [Diego d'Azevedo], his bishop, chose him as companion on an embassy to Denmark to arrange a

marriage for the son of King Alfonso VIII of Castile. In passing through southern France, the travelers came to know the Albigensian heretics; in fact, the innkeeper where they stayed on their first night was a member of the sect. Dominic's zeal for souls, which had ripened during his years of contemplative life . . . burst into flame. He stayed up all night arguing with his host. With the rising of the sun, the man gave up his heresy and returned to the Catholic faith. (William A. Hinnebusch, *The Dominicans: A Short History*, p. 6)

Receiving the gift of speaking in an unfamiliar language is among the legends about Dominic. While he was on a journey, a group of German pilgrims gave gracious hospitality to Dominic and another friar. Determined to show his appreciation to the Germans for their kindness, Dominic offered them the greatest gift he could imagine—he preached for them.

While travelling from Toulouse to Paris in company with Brother Bertrand de Garrigue, who was the first Provincial of Provence, our holy father spent the night in watching and prayer in the church of our Lady at Roc-Amadour. Next day they came up with a band of pilgrims from Germany, who, hearing them reciting the Psalms and Litanies, joined company with them, and on coming to the next town hospitably entertained them during three days. One morning St Dominic addressed Brother Bertrand after this fashion: "Good brother, I am much troubled in conscience seeing that we are reaping the material good things of these pilgrims without sowing spiritual ones in return, so, if it please you, let us kneel down and ask God to enable us to understand their tongue, that we may preach Jesus Christ to them." This they did, and to the bewilderment of the pilgrims they began to speak fluently in German, and as they trudged along together during the next four days, they continued conversing about our Lord Jesus Christ until they came to Orleans. There the Germans, who were on their way to Chartres, parted company with them on the road which led to Paris, after humbly commending themselves to their prayers. Some time after this our holy father said to

Brother Bertrand: "Brother, we are now going to enter Paris, and if our brethren here only knew of that miracle which God wrought in us they would repute us to be saints, whereas we are but sinners, and if it got rumoured abroad we should be liable to vanity: wherefore, in virtue of holy obedience I forbid you to mention it to a soul until after my death." Nor was it divulged to our brethren until after his death. (Placid Conway, trans., and Bede Jarrett, ed., *Lives of the Brethren of the Order of Preachers: 1206–1259*, pp. 49–50)

Pause: Consider how you promote the Gospel message simply by the way you interact with people throughout a typical day.

Dominic's Words

For Dominic, Jesus' words from Luke's Gospel served as the model for the way in which his brothers and sisters should preach:

Jesus appointed seventy-two preachers and sent them out in pairs to all the villages and other spots that he would soon be visiting. Before they departed, he gave them these instructions: "The harvest is rich but the farm hands are few. Ask God who gives the harvest to add to your numbers. Go forth now, but be alert. You are lambs among wolves. Don't burden yourselves with excess baggage. Wear no sandals. On the road, pray and stay silent. Whenever you arrive at a house, greet the people living there by proclaiming, 'Peace be to this house!' If peaceful people reside there, your peace will settle among them. If they are not peaceful, your peace will remain with you. Enjoy what food and drink they share with you. Workers deserve their wages. Do not shift from house to house. Now when you go into a town where people make you welcome, eat what they offer you. Cure the sick folks, and tell them, 'The Reign of God is very close to you.' On the other hand, if townspeople do not welcome you, go out in public and declare, 'We shake the dust of your town off of our feet. Take heed: the Reign of God is very close to you.' I assure you, on the Day of Judgment, that town will be treated worse than Sodom." (Adapted from Luke 10:1–12)

Reflection

Dominic founded the Order of Preachers to engage primarily in what has been called doctrinal preaching—that is, formal preaching (usually at worship events) in which specific aspects of Christian theology are clarified. However, Dominic evangelized in many other ways.

By his daily example, Dominic engaged in the "living preaching" that Christians may do by loving their neighbors as themselves. When Dominic taught or explained faith in conversation, which he did often, he shared in the catechetical form of the church's preaching mission. When he affirmed the goodness he found in other people, he proclaimed Christ in a way called exhortative preaching.

What Dominicans call the Holy Preaching assumes any of these forms: formal preaching, living preaching, catechetical instruction, or exhortation. Following Jesus' example, Dominic called believers to participate in the Holy Preaching using the form most suited to their way of life. Even though Dominicans specifically belong to the Order of Preachers, all baptized Christians belong to a universal community of preachers.

✧ Read the section "Dominic's Words" again slowly and meditatively. Imagine that you are one of the seventy-two preachers that Jesus is sending out. What are your feelings about this mission being given to you? What physical, spiritual, or emotional baggage will you have to leave behind? Do you really want to go on this mission?

Then, recalling that Jesus is present with you, prayerfully respond to the following questions:

✦ Do I really believe that Jesus calls me to preach now, today?

✦ If I do believe that I am called, what baggage do I carry that hinders me from proclaiming God's peace to people?

✦ What grace do I need from God to be a preaching disciple of Jesus?

✧ Find the Gospel passage that will be used in next Sunday's worship at your church. Try to read the passage at least once daily before Sunday. As the week progresses, think about how you would preach this Gospel selection if you were the preacher at your church on Sunday. What theme would you highlight? What stories from your own experiences would you use to give the passage immediacy?

Not only is this a helpful way to pray with the Scriptures, but it will also engage you more fully when you are worshiping on Sunday. The intimacy you will have developed with the Gospel passage throughout the week can help you enter more completely into the celebration of the word.

✧ Read the selection from the Gospel of Matthew in the "God's Word" section of this meditation. For Christians, each day is filled with numerous opportunities to give witness to the Gospel message. Pray with these questions:

✦ If every moment is an opportunity to give witness or preach that Jesus is the Good News, what does my giving witness or preaching look like today?

✦ What choices have I made today that have given witness to Gospel values?

✦ Am I aware of my own resistance to any opportunities to promote Gospel harmony?

✦ How is the world a more just and peaceful place in which to live because of my actions?

✧ Pray for the people who have preached the Gospel to you by the example of their life. Ask yourself:

✦ Who are the genuinely good, holy people in my life?

✦ What is it about their goodness that touches me?

✦ Am I able to integrate more of that goodness into my own life? How?

Conclude by making a prayer of thanksgiving for the goodness of these persons.

If possible, express your gratitude and affirmation to these special people in some way.

✧ In the evening, look ahead to the following day. What kinds of encounters do you anticipate? What sorts of activities will be part of your day tomorrow? Reflect on how you can approach each situation in light of the Gospel. Plan your day and then check out your plans with Jesus.

God's Word

Jesus came up and spoke to them. He said, "All authority in heaven and on earth has been given to me. Go, therefore, make disciples of all nations; baptise them in the name of the Father and of the Son and of the Holy Spirit, and teach them to observe all the commands I gave you. And look, I am with you always; yes, to the end of time." (Matthew 28:18–20)

Closing prayer:

Lord,
let the holiness and teaching of St. Dominic
come to the aid of your Church.
May he help us now with his prayers
as he once inspired people by his preaching.
(*The Roman Missal*, Feast of St. Dominic, p. 680)

✧ Meditation 2 ✧

Sacred Study

Theme: Dominic grew increasingly aware that widespread ignorance and misunderstanding of the Christian faith prevented many of his contemporaries from growing in intimacy with God. He also knew that anyone who wanted to preach God's word effectively had to know what they were talking about. Accordingly, Dominic committed himself to lifelong study of the Scriptures and Christian tradition, and he urged his followers to do the same.

Opening prayer: Loving God, draw me into a more intense relationship with you as I grow to know you better by studying about you and your creation.

About Dominic

Humbert of Romans, the third master general of the Dominicans, remarked that "'study is not the object of the Order, but is absolutely necessary for the accomplishing of the aforesaid object (namely, preaching and the saving of souls), which cannot be achieved without study'" (Jarrett, *Life,* p. 98). Dominic himself made study an essential element in his own life.

Dominic's study fed not only his mind but his relationship with God. Indeed, his study of the Scriptures and Christian tradition became a form of prayer for him.

The holy father Dominic also had another beautiful way of praying, full of devotion and grace. After the canonical Hours and the grace which is said in common after meals, the father would go off quickly on his own to a cell or somewhere, sober and alert and anointed with a spirit of devotion which he had drawn from the divine words which had been sung in choir or during the meal; there he would sit down to read or pray, recollecting himself in himself and fixing himself in the presence of God. Sitting there quietly he would open some book before him, arming himself first with the sign of the cross, and then he would read. And he would be moved in his mind as delightfully as if he heard the Lord speaking to him. As the Psalm says, "I will hear what the Lord God is saying in me." It was as if he were arguing with a friend; at one moment he would appear to be feeling impatient, nodding his head energetically, then he would seem to be listening quietly, then you would see him disputing and struggling, and laughing and weeping all at once, fixing his gaze, submitting, then again speaking quietly and beating his breast. If anyone was inquisitive enough to want to spy on him secretly, he would find that the holy father Dominic was like Moses, who went into the innermost desert and saw the burning bush and the Lord speaking and calling to him to humble himself. The man of God had a prophetic way of passing quickly from reading to prayer and from meditation to contemplation. (Simon Tugwell, ed., *Early Dominicans: Selected Writings*, p. 101)

Pause: Ponder the role that study of the Scriptures and Christian tradition play in your spirituality.

Dominic's Words

Among Dominic's followers today, one of the favorite likenesses of him is a detail of a Fra Angelico masterpiece that shows Dominic seated on the floor studying with an open book in his lap. Dominicans enjoy this image because it highlights an aspect of Dominic's life that they cherish—Dominic at study.

The inadequate theological training of preachers proved to be a primary source of the faith crisis in the church during Dominic's life. Determined that his fledgling band of preachers would be prepared adequately for their sacred mission, he mandated that religious study be a daily, rigorous, and integral part of life for members of his community. Stories tell of Dominic leading his companions to the daily lectures of Master Alexander Stavensby, who taught at the cathedral school of Toulouse. Other friars recorded that from time to time, Dominic would move among the community encouraging them to celebrate the Divine Office with spirit and dispatch. This pattern of worship made greater opportunity for study possible. While monks spent time at prayer and manual labor, the friars devoted themselves to study.

Dominic's emphasis on study later became established in the community's constitution. Study assumed such importance for the friars that they could presume to absent themselves from the community prayer services if study could not be conveniently interrupted. Furthermore, student friars were not assigned regular household duties that might impede their intellectual endeavors. Whereas members generally slept in large dormitories, those who studied into the night could be assigned private rooms. Custom dictated that a director of studies be appointed for every community of preachers so that each house was, in effect, a school of theology.

The instructions given to directors responsible for training the newest members of the community make explicit Dominic's belief in the power and importance of study:

> Teach them how earnest they must be in their study, always reading or thinking about something by day and by night, in the house and when they are on a journey, and striving to retain as much as they can in their minds. (Tugwell, *Early Dominicans*, p. 466)

Reflection

Thinking of study time as worship of God may seem odd at first. However, Dominic understood that whenever we better understand the created world, its resources and its inhabitants, the better we know the Creator. The better we know the Creator, the deeper our intimacy with God will become.

Sacred study can be compared to growing in friendship. When we first meet people, we usually try to find out as much as we can about them. We might start by learning some essential data—their name, job, interests, and so on. Over time, people may reveal more subtle or private things—their beliefs, ideals, foibles, dislikes, moods, and so on. Eventually, our study of a person, who by now is a friend, will lead us to profound empathy. Often at this level of intimacy or deep learning, our will, dreams, and intentions become united with those of the other person.

Dominic realized that study of the word of God and Christian tradition could lead his friars into a deeper friendship with God. Through study, they would learn more and more about Jesus, the perfect revelation of God. They would also learn about the many ways in which God is constantly revealed in the natural world. Increased understanding of God would then engender closer intimacy with God. With this intimacy, they could effectively proclaim God's great love for all humanity.

Dominic invites all of us to make study a part of our spiritual life. When we listen to God speaking to us during study, we deepen our relationship with the source of all wisdom and love.

✧ One way of doing sacred study is outlined here:
1. Place yourself in God's presence.
2. Slowly and prayerfully read this scriptural passage:

> My dear friends,
> let us love each other,
> since love is from God
> and everyone who loves is a child of God and knows God.
> (1 John 4:7)

3. Ask yourself: What is God trying to say to me personally and intimately through this verse? How do I feel moved to respond to God's message?

4. Study this commentary on the verse from the First Letter of John:

> "Everyone who loves . . . knows God"—that is the song of the Apostle John (1 Jn 4:7). That knowledge is made of flesh and blood. The way of the knowledge of God will always be the roundabout one of human history and that of the histories of individual people. Since Christ's coming, there are no longer two sides: one of the eternal Word and the other of our stammerings. At the heart of the new covenant there is Jesus Christ, the Word of God and our flesh. The words that are on our lips are God's words. They are appeal and communion, cry and song. That is because the Word perpetuates in each individual person the history of Emmanuel, God-with-us. (Marcel Bastin, Ghislain Pinckers, and Michel Teheux, *God Day by Day: Following the Weekday Lectionary*, trans. David Smith, vol. 4, p. 71)

5. Return to the scriptural passage. Read it again. Allow the information from the commentary to influence your understanding of the text. Allow the text itself to form your prayer conversation with God. How is the Spirit of God speaking to you through this reading?

6. After finishing your reflection, remain seated quietly for several moments before returning to the day's activities.

✧ Slowly pray the Lord's Prayer, trying to understand each phrase in a new and deeper way. Consulting a commentary might prove helpful in your study.

✧ Another type of sacred study comes in the form of examining the events of daily life. Peruse today's newspaper, offering a prayer at each headline that strikes you. For instance, a story about a military conflict may cause you to offer a prayer for peace, or a headline describing human suffering could well move you to pray for the alleviation of that suffering. As you scan the newspaper and become informed about world conditions, ask Jesus what he wants you to learn from these events and how he wants you to respond.

✧ Read a story about some scientific discovery or technological breakthrough. Whether this is unfamiliar or familiar territory for you, ask for God's guidance that you might see the mystery and power of God in a new way. Recall that the Creator is revealed throughout all of creation. Meditate on the new discovery or breakthrough, and ask God what it means for humanity and what it reveals about the Creator.

✧ Religious study may be done in a variety of ways: by reading Christian periodicals, books, commentaries, or texts; by attending faith-sharing groups, talks, or presentations; or simply by praying with the Scriptures, perhaps in consultation with a commentary.

Reflect on each of these questions in dialog with Jesus:

✦ Do I feel a need to study God's word and Christian tradition more fully?

✦ Are there particular questions about God and living as a Christian that have gone unanswered for me long enough? (If so, list some questions requiring study.)

✦ Realistically, what can I do to become a better student of my faith and of God's actions in all of life?

God's Word

"Come to me, all you who labour and are overburdened, and I will give you rest. Shoulder my yoke and learn from me, for I am gentle and humble in heart, and you will find rest for your souls. Yes, my yoke is easy and my burden light." (Matthew 11:28–30)

Closing prayer: God of creation, you have revealed yourself to humanity through your word in human history. Instill within me a desire to see you more clearly every time I encounter you in your word, your people, and the other wonders of life. Bless me with the spirit of inquiry and the discipline to channel that inquiry into a lifelong pursuit of your Divine Self.

✧ **Meditation 3** ✧

Putting on the Truth

Theme: Dominic realized that in order to preach the Truth, he first had to understand and "put on" that Truth. Dominic passionately wanted to clothe himself with Jesus Christ, the divine truth. Putting on the Truth entails more than studying doctrine. Dominic sought to integrate the truths of the Gospel into the fabric of his life.

Opening prayer: Loving God, instill within me the same passion for truth that characterized Saint Dominic's life. May I grow in deeper intimacy with you as I grow in my awareness and understanding of you, who are Truth itself.

About Dominic

Dominic understood Christ's words to be the source of truth. This story reveals Dominic's radical passion for studying and then for living Christ's truth as he understood it.

At the conclusion of the ordinary lesson, the master condensed his teaching in brief explanatory phrases, the glosses, which he put before his students. Dominic would write them down on his tablets. To ponder more deeply on their meaning, when he got back to his room he would copy them carefully into the parchment notebooks in which he had the text of the Bible copied by a scribe. Thus

41

he had his real treasure in his own home—the books covered with glosses which preserved for him both the word of God and the instrument to penetrate the riches of it. (P. 28)

In the Gospel over which he spent his vigils he read: "If thou wilt be perfect, go, sell all thou hast and give to the poor." (P. 30)

Dominic, too, in Palencia, saw people perishing of hunger. Hardly anyone among the rich or the authorities came to their help. He could bear it no longer. "Touched by the distress of the poor and yearning with compassion, he resolved by one single action to obey the evangelical counsels and to relieve the wretchedness of the poor who were perishing, with all his power." Establishing a "charity" forthwith, he divided his possessions and gave them to the poor. . . .

. . . He sold even his manuscripts, those manuscripts written on parchment, annotated with his own hand, . . . "I will not study on dead skins when men are dying of hunger." . . . In a certain sense he sacrificed the life of his mind in the face of his neighbour's urgent distress. (M.-H. Vicaire, *Saint Dominic and His Times*, trans. Kathleen Pond, pp. 29–30)

Pause: Ponder this question: How strong is my desire to study and put on the Truth?

Dominic's Words

Albigensianism alienated people from many Gospel values and wreaked havoc in Dominic's society. The cultists believed that whereas spiritual beings came from God, material beings were the handiwork of an evil god. Therefore, they concluded that human life was intrinsically evil. This resulted in an exaggerated system of discipline and penance.

Dedicated to whipping their own flesh into submission, Albigensian preachers practiced a conspicuously severe poverty of lifestyle. By contrast, the papal legates and preachers sent to contest the Albigensians seemed rich, indulgent, and haughty to the unlettered, impoverished common folk of the time, among whom the Albigensians made many converts.

Dominic knew that personal example had to accompany the word of God that he preached. Dominic's study of the Gospels showed him that preachers could give credible witness to the poor Christ only when they themselves lived in simplicity and poverty. As a result, Dominic required that his preaching band dress simply and beg for food and lodging. Just as Jesus had no wealth, neither did the preaching friars. According to some accounts, Dominic summarized his views about putting on Christ this way:

> "Zeal must be met by zeal," . . . "lowliness by lowliness, false sanctity by real sanctity, preaching lies by preaching truth." (M. Assumpta O'Hanlon, *St. Dominic: Servant but Friend*, p. 45)

Knowing the content of the Scriptures was necessary, but putting on Jesus Christ demanded behavior in daily life consistent with Jesus' words. Only Christlike behavior would give effective witness to other people.

Reflection

Dominic "took it for granted that to introduce [people] to Truth was to lead them directly to all virtue" (John-Baptist Reeves, *The Dominicans*, p. 68). He knew that Jesus is the Way, the Truth, and the Life.

Without the Truth that calls us to justice, peacemaking, hope, and love, only conflict, dissension, alienation, oppression, and violence can emerge within a community.

Dominic's constant theme that has influenced the minds and hearts of his followers for eight centuries has been *veritas*, or truth. Dominic understood well that the chains enslaving people—addiction, hate, greed, ignorance, vanity—could be broken only by the truth that would set them free, the truth contained in the person of Jesus. Because Jesus is encountered in the Gospel, it must be heard, studied, and understood, and then it must be put on as the fabric of our life. When we put on Christ, we put on the Truth.

✧ Consider one important decision you are facing. Now, reflect on who and what are involved in the decision. Ask yourself, What values are at stake in this decision?

Recollect stories from the Gospels that shed light on your decision. Peruse the Gospel of Matthew for words of Jesus that apply to your decision. Meditate on any passages that seem to apply.

Finally, converse with Jesus about your decision. Place your considerations or plan of action before Jesus, asking him to respond and critique your discernment.

✧ If Jesus were to sit down with you right now, what would he tell you about your positive attributes? Next, what would Jesus say are your blind spots, your addictions, or your areas of sinfulness? Ask Jesus any questions that come to mind. Listen to his responses. Then slowly and meditatively repeat this prayer over and over: "The Truth will set me free." You may find it helpful to write down this conversation.

✧ Look through the day's newspaper or a current news magazine. As you find various accounts of injustice and suffering, ponder how the absence of Gospel truth has led to this situation. Is greed, the drive for personal power, or a lack of concern for poor or victimized people the cause of this problem?

Identify the truth that is lacking and pray that this truth will emerge.

✧ A word similar to *truth* is *humility*. Humility is an honest recognition of who we are before God and our brothers and sisters. After you read each of the Beatitudes in Luke 6:20–23, meditate on the statement following it. Recalling that the truth sets us free, pray each of the Beatitudes this way:

"How blessed are you who are poor: the [Reign] of God is yours." God, bless me because I am poor in these ways: . . . May I come into your Reign.

"Blessed are you who are hungry now: you shall have your fill." Dear God, you know that I am hungry for: . . . Please, give me my fill of your living water and eternal food.

"Blessed are you who are weeping now: you shall laugh." You, God, know that I weep about: . . . Bless me with laughter.

"Blessed are you when people hate you, drive you out, abuse you, denounce your name as criminal, on account of the Son. . . . Rejoice when that day comes and dance for joy, look!—your reward will be great in heaven." These, merciful God, are the ways in which I am hated, abused, rejected, and ridiculed because of my love for you: . . . Set my heart to dancing and bring me to my reward with you!

✧ In Matthew, Dominic's favorite Gospel, Jesus says,

"'Human beings live not on bread alone,
but on every word that comes from the mouth of God.'"
(4:4)

Jesus is the word of God; we are called to become the word of God in our world. Meditate on these questions:
+ Have I tried to live on bread alone?
+ What words of Jesus do I resist speaking and acting out in my daily life?
+ What words of Jesus do I desperately want to speak in words and deeds?

God's Word

Jesus says:
"If you make my word your home
you will indeed be my disciples;
you will come to know the truth,
and the truth will set you free."

(John 8:31–32)

Closing prayer: O Holy One, send your Holy Spirit upon me so that each day I may be attentive to your word in my life and be ever ready to live out the implications of your call. I sincerely pray that I may put on Jesus who is the Way, the Truth, and the Life.

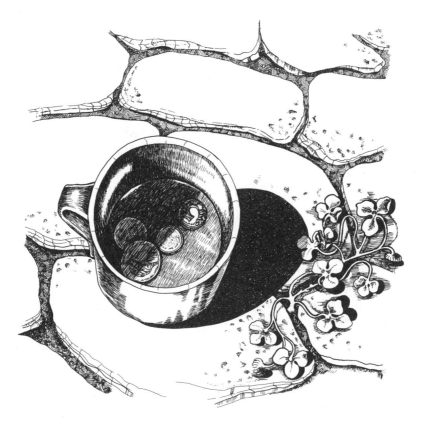

✧ **Meditation 4** ✧

To Praise, to Bless

Theme: "To praise, to bless, to preach" is an important Dominican motto. In addition to preaching, the acts of praising and blessing God's name root us in a relationship with God, the source of all strength and wisdom.

Opening prayer: Most Holy Trinity, may all praise, all honor, and all glory be yours, now and forever.

About Dominic

As a young canon at Osma, Dominic committed himself to a contemplative community of clerics whose primary responsibility was to sing God's praises throughout the day at the local cathedral. Typical of contemplative communities, the canons of Osma had limited responsibility for active, pastoral ministries. Theirs was primarily a ministry of praise.

At the age of thirty-four, when Dominic left the quiet of the cathedral walls to embark upon the preaching mission that became his life's work, he never abandoned his commitment to praising, blessing, and contemplating.

Dominic's companions recorded his lifelong commitment to the praise of God. While traveling, Dominic prayed constantly. At home and on the road, he spent his nights in marathons of praise and adoration. He also insisted that the preaching community pray the prayer of the church, the Liturgy of the Hours. In this way, they would join the universal church in ceaselessly singing God's praises through the Psalms.

The simple rules guiding Dominican prayer are taken from the Rule of Saint Augustine, which Dominic selected for his community:

1. "Persevere in prayer" (Col. 4:2) at the hours and times appointed.
2. In the oratory no one should do anything out of keeping with the purpose of the place. So that if some perhaps have leisure and wish to pray outside the regular hours, they should not be distracted. . . .
3. When with Psalms and hymns you pray to God, ponder in your heart what your voice utters.

(Mary T. Clark, trans.,
Augustine of Hippo: Selected Writings, p. 486)

His attitude toward prayer has been described this way:

We may not neglect the souls of others, but our first concern is with our own. . . . To Dominic it seemed that the preacher needed to be immersed in the things of the spirit before he could hope to convince and stir the hearts of others. (Jarrett, *Life*, pp. 99–100)

Although the Holy Preaching was Dominic's mission, he understood clearly that effective preaching resulted from and led to a life of praise and blessing.

Pause: Ask yourself, How does the praise of God and the blessing of God's holy name find its place in my prayer life?

Dominic's Words

The culture would allow only men to roam about as itinerant preachers, so the contemplative nuns took part in the community's mission by continually praising God in prayer.

The only extant material written by Dominic himself is a letter to contemplative women living in Madrid. In this brief letter, Dominic manifests his attitude about founding another house of praise and blessing. Dominic wrote:

> I am delighted at the fervour with which you follow your holy way of life, and thank God for it. He has indeed freed you. . . .
>
> Fight the good fight, my daughters, against our ancient foe . . . because no one will win the crown of victory without engaging in the contest in the proper way.
>
> Until now you had no place where you could practise your religious life, but now . . . by the grace of God, you have buildings that are quite suitable enough for religious observance. (Tugwell, *Early Dominicans*, p. 394)

Within the enclosure of their new buildings, the nuns praised and blessed God. This weekday preface from *The Roman Missal* neatly expresses why praising and blessing God supplies strength and wisdom for ministry:

> All-powerful and ever-living God,
> we do well always and everywhere to give you thanks.

> You have no need of our praise,
> yet our desire to thank you is itself your gift.
> Our prayer of thanksgiving adds nothing to your
>   greatness,
> but makes us grow in your grace,
> through Jesus Christ.
>
> (The Roman Missal, p. 453)

Reflection

Some ways to establish positive relationships with people are to show interest in, care for, and affirm them. Accordingly, to praise and to bless are natural responses to the constant invitation to be in relationship with God.

When we recognize that God loves us unconditionally, we grow in God's grace. The act of naming God's gifts to us reminds us that God is always with us. God does not need to be reminded that God loves us; we need the reminder. By praising God for any life experience—a rich harvest, a particularly loving friend, or a pain that has taught us patience—we remind ourselves of God's abiding love.

Praising and blessing God is ancient. One of the clearest manifestations of this form of prayer is the Book of Psalms. Another prayer of blessing in the Jewish tradition is the *berakah*. This prayer form invariably begins, "Blessed be Yahweh . . . " and then continues in praise and blessing of God according to the particular theme of each prayer.

By praising and blessing God, we dispose ourselves for a deeper relationship with God, the source of our courage, wisdom, hope, and love, without which meaningful ministry is impossible.

✧ What are the signs in your life that indicate God's goodness and grandeur surrounds you? Make a mental or written inventory of these blessings, and praise God for each gift.

✧ Prayerfully ponder the preface prayer in the "Dominic's Words" section of this meditation. Reflect on how praising and thanking your Holy Friend has helped you grow in grace.

✧ Pray this poem by Gerard Manley Hopkins and then meditate on the images in it.

> Glory be to God for dappled things—
> > For skies of couple-colour as a brinded cow;
> > > For rose-moles all in stipple upon trout that
> > > swim;
> Fresh-firecoal chestnut-falls; finches' wings;
> > Landscape plotted and pieced—fold, fallow, and
> > > plough;
> > > And áll trádes, their gear and tackle and trim.
>
> All things counter, original, spare, strange;
> > Whatever is fickle, freckled (who knows how?)
> > > With swift, slow; sweet, sour; adazzle, dim;
> He fathers-forth whose beauty is past change:
> > Praise him.
> > > (Gerard Manley Hopkins, "Pied Beauty")

Look out the window of your house or apartment, sit on your porch or in your yard, or go for a walk. Gaze at all of God's gifts; name each gift and praise God for it.

✧ Recall something unpleasant that happened to you recently—maybe an argument with a friend or perhaps some accident. Have you grown through this event? Praise and thank God for the growth that has taken place because of this unpleasant occurrence. Say your prayer of praise and thanks several times. Finally, converse with God about these questions:

+ Was it difficult to praise and thank God for these unpleasant things? If so, why?
+ What good came or could come from praising and thanking God for what is uncomfortable in your life?
+ How can difficulties be gifts?

✧ Read the psalm in the "God's Word" section of this meditation. After praying God's psalm, make up your own psalm of praise, naming other gifts from God that are important to you right now.

✧ Pray the Gloria in the "Closing prayer" section of this meditation. Try to pray the Gloria throughout your day.

God's Word

Praise God from the heavens;
praise God in the heights;
praise God, all you angels;
praise God, all you heavenly hosts.
Praise God, sun and moon;
praise God, all you shining stars.
Praise God, you highest heavens,
and you waters above the heavens.
Let them praise the name of God,
who commanded and they were created.
God established them forever and ever
and gave a decree which shall not pass away.

Praise God all the earth,
you sea monsters and all depths,
fire and hail, snow and mist,
storm winds that fulfill God's word.
You mountains and all you hills,
you fruit trees and all you cedars,
you wild beasts and all tame animals,
you creeping things and flying birds.
Let the rulers of the earth and all peoples
and all the judges of the earth—
young men too, and maidens,
old women and men—
praise the name of God
whose name alone is exalted;
whose majesty is above earth and heaven,
and who has raised the fortunes of the people.
Be this God praised by all the faithful ones,
by the children of Israel, the people close to God.
Alleluia.

(Psalm 148)

Closing prayer:

Glory to God in the highest,
and peace to his people on earth.

Lord God, heavenly King,
almighty God and Father,
    we worship you, we give you thanks,
    we praise you for your glory.

Lord Jesus Christ, only Son of the Father,
Lord God, Lamb of God,
you take away the sin of the world:
    have mercy on us;
you are seated at the right hand of the Father:
    receive our prayer.

For you alone are the Holy One,
you alone are the Lord,

you alone are the Most High,
    Jesus Christ,
    with the Holy Spirit,
    in the glory of God the Father. Amen.
                               (*The Roman Missal*, p. 365)

✧ Meditation 5 ✧

Movement as Adoration

Theme: For Dominic, adoration of God involved his entire being, even his body.

Opening prayer: O Divine Companion, help me to offer myself totally to you. I love you and adore you with all of my being.

About Dominic

In the style of stories told about saints at the time, these stories give some indication of Dominic's active prayer life:

Brother John of Bologna . . . tells us how he [Brother John] once kept diligent watch for seven succeeding nights, in order to see for himself in what manner [Dominic] used to spend his night watches. This is how he describes it. "Standing at one time and groaning heavily, or with his face down upon the church pavement, he prolonged his prayer until sleep overcame him. Then starting up he would visit each altar in turn, and so kept on until midnight, when he would softly visit the sleeping brethren and cover them up when he saw fit." This same brother tells how when serving [Dominic's] mass he often saw the tears trickle from his eyes down his cheeks as he turned to [wash his hands] after receiving the Body of Christ. (Conway and Jarrett, *Lives of the Brethren*, pp. 53–54)

After Dominic's death, friends and community members treasured their recollections of his prayerful habits. One person recalled, "'I never saw anyone pray so much, nor anyone who wept so much. And when he was at prayer he used to pray so loudly that he could be heard everywhere'" (p. 6). Another added:

> But also, at times, he spoke in his heart and his voice was not heard at all, and he would remain on his knees, his mind caught up in wonder, and this sometimes lasted a long time. Sometimes, when he was praying like this, his gaze seemed to have penetrated into the spiritual heavens, and he would suddenly be radiant with joy, wiping away the abundant tears running down his face. At such times he would be in an intensity of desire, like a thirsty man coming to a spring of water, or a traveller at last approaching his homeland. His prayer became stronger and more insistent, his movements rapid yet always sure and orderly, as he stood up and knelt down. (Simon Tugwell, ed. and trans., *The Nine Ways of Prayer of Saint Dominic,* pp. 26–28)

Pause: Ponder this question: How do I feel about bodily expression in movement during my prayer?

Dominic's Words

After Dominic's death, his custom of physical prayer was recorded in a small book entitled *The Nine Ways of Prayer of Saint Dominic.* In most of the nine ways, Dominic is depicted as employing physical postures and movement to prayerfully encounter God:

> Sometimes, when he wanted to teach the brethren with what reverence they ought to pray, he would say to them: "the Magi, those holy kings, fell down and worshipped when they entered the house and found the child with Mary his mother. Now we know for certain that we have found him too, man and God; . . . so come, let us worship and fall down before God, let us weep before the God who made us." (Tugwell, *The Nine Ways,* p. 18)

When Dominic used the words *worship, fall down,* and *weep,* he was using these words literally. He urged his followers to worship using literally their whole body.

Dominic would sometimes prostrate himself on the floor in a gesture of humility and beseech God's mercy for himself and others. Other times, he would genuflect or bow deeply repeatedly to signify humility before God. Many of these movements could be incorporated into modern liturgical dance.

Occasionally Dominic would stretch his entire body heavenward, an emotional and physical gesture revealing his intense passion for union with God. His custom of standing before the crucifix with his own arms pointed outward at each side, reproducing Christ's own posture on the cross, further shows Dominic's yearning for intimacy with the Divine One.

Dominic strove to love God with his whole mind, his whole spirit, and his whole body.

Reflection

For people used to a more sedate or cerebral way of praying, Dominic's highly emotional and active manner may seem exaggerated or even distasteful. However, Dominic and many of the other holy people of his age, like Francis of Assisi for instance, were passionate men and women of faith whose prayer and adoration took many forms.

Because prayer is such an intimate activity, experimenting with different and unfamiliar prayer forms can be unsettling. Nonetheless, human nature is complex, and integrating many facets of the human experience into prayer life can be rewarding, invigorating, and deepening.

God created us whole human beings: emotions, intellect, will, body, and spirit. From the beginning we have been invited to love God and our brothers and sisters as whole human beings. Prayer, so integral to nurturing our love of God, can best be done when we commit our entire self to it. Dominic realized this, and prayed this way.

✧ Try this:

1. Allow both of your arms to relax at your sides with your hands open, fingers pointing downward and your palms facing forward.
2. Raise your hands, lifting them forward about six inches, with an open, inviting gesture, as you would imagine Christ saying, "Come to me."
3. Hold this position a few moments. Notice how you feel.
4. Now flip your palms so they are facing downward. Bend your elbows and raise your hands to shoulder height, so that your fingers are pointing upward and your palms are facing outward again. You have assumed the posture of repelling whomever is approaching you.
5. How does this posture feel?
6. Change back and forth between the two postures several times.
7. Note any differences in feelings that the two postures evoke in you.
8. Once again, assume the first posture of open hands, and prayerfully invite God into your whole being. Linger with the Divine for as long as you wish.

Writing your reflections on this prayer of movement and each of the subsequent ones in a journal may lead to new insights.

✧ In your prayer space:

1. Kneel down, sitting on your heels, in front of a favorite symbol or image of God, an open book of the sacred Scriptures, or a candle.
2. While offering adoration, praise, and thanksgiving to the Divine One present with you, bend forward until your forehead touches the floor in front of you.
3. Allow yourself to remain in this position as long as you desire.

✧ Again, in the presence of an image or symbol, pray the Jesus Prayer over and over again, using it as a mantra: "Lord Jesus Christ, Son of God, be merciful to me, a sinner." If you feel free to do so, chant or pray aloud. Pray the words slowly, relishing the sound of each word. If you feel so moved, extend your arms in the shape of a cross, letting your body assume the form of the crucified Jesus.

✧ Modify the Jesus Prayer to reflect more accurately your relationship with Christ. For instance, feeling the need for peace, you might pray, "Jesus, prince of peace, have mercy on me, a sinner." As you pray the Jesus Prayer, you may eventually find yourself just praying the holy name *Jesus*.

✧ In a space where you can enjoy freedom of movement and as much privacy as you feel you need, play a recording of a song or instrumental piece that stirs you. Recall God's presence dwelling within you. Then, allow your body to move, dance, and respond to the music in any way you feel. Your dance is your prayer.

✧ Traditionally, spiritual directors have reminded us of the power of the sense of smell. During your prayer time, light some incense. Incense powerfully supports the meditative experience. Or, if you have a favorite flower, place it near your place of prayer so you can enjoy its fragrance.

✧ Sing to God a special hymn. If you know and like it, "The Lord of the Dance" would be appropriate.

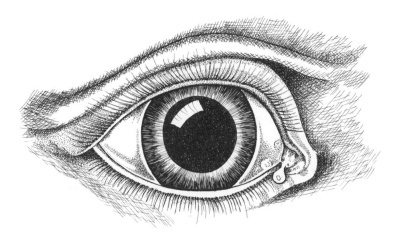

God's Word

One thing have I asked of you, Yahweh,
this I seek:
to dwell in your house
all the days of my life,
to behold your beauty
and to contemplate on your Temple.

. . . .

I will offer in your tent
sacrifices with shouts of joy;
I will sing and make melody to you.
Hear me when I cry aloud;
be gracious to me and answer me!
You have said, "Seek my face."
My heart says to you, "Your face I do seek."

(Psalm 27:4–8)

Closing prayer: God of movement and stillness, song and silence, excitement and tranquillity, help me to see that all movement offered to you is itself an act of worship before you. May every word I utter become a song of praise, every thought I entertain become a meditation, every step I take become a dance in your honor.

✧ **Meditation 6** ✧

Prayerful Journeys

Theme: As Dominic made his preaching journeys, he used the time walking between towns as an opportunity to pray. He not only praised and thanked God but conversed with God about what he should say to the people.

Opening prayer: Divine Companion, be with me and guide me as I go about my activities today. Help me to grow in my awareness of your constant presence and love in my life.

About Dominic

Journeyings were a necessity of his way, and they were undertaken in the same spirit of joy as had always marked with charm his manner of serving God. The chronicles tell of his passing over Europe, reading as he strode along the roads, talking of divine things as he toiled staff in hand to his newly rising convents, and in the lightness of his heart singing hymns and antiphons. This is the picture of the saint on which, perhaps, the imagination best loves to dwell; . . . we watch him striding steadfastly the highways of Christendom and filling all Europe with his song. (Jarrett, *Life,* p. 98)

Pause: Reflect on the ways you are mindful of God's presence in the movement of your day.

Dominic's Words

After Dominic's death, his followers included prayerful travel as one of the Nine Ways of Prayer:

> This way of prayer he used to observe when he was going from one country to another, especially when he was in a lonely place. . . . Sometimes he would say to his travelling companions, "It is written in Hosea, 'I will lead her into the wilderness and speak to her heart.'" So sometimes he went aside from his companion or went on ahead or, more often, lingered far behind; going on on his own he would pray as he walked, and a fire was kindled in his meditation. . . . The brethren thought that in this kind of prayer the saint acquired the fulness of sacred scripture and the very heart of the understanding of God's words, and also a power and boldness to preach fervently, and a hidden intimacy with the Holy Spirit to know hidden things. (Tugwell, *Early Dominicans*, p. 102)

Reflection

Dominic spent much of his life walking from place to place in Europe. His frequent journeys were walking tours with God, the ever-present and faithful companion without whom no journey could succeed. God travels with us on every journey we make, whether it be from place to place or from moment to moment. After all, from a Christian perspective, life is a pilgrimage with God. The same God who walked with Dominic walks with us this day.

Dominic's journey turned into prayer because he acknowledged the presence of his Divine Companion. Dominic thanked his Companion and asked for his Friend's advice and direction.

On our pilgrimage through life, God lives with us and in us and in every aspect of life, no matter how seemingly mundane or insignificant. Each mile or moment in the journey presents an opportunity to encounter God. In fact, God awaits us specifically in the ordinary routines of life. Like Dominic, we need only invite God to be our constant companion.

✧ Recall the people you've encountered and the events in which you've participated in the last twenty-four hours. Then reflect on these questions:

✦ How was God present to you through the persons and events that come to mind?

✦ Has God been more involved in the day's events than you originally thought?

✦ What is it about certain people that enables them to grace a gathering with a sense of the goodness, kindness, and sensitivity that are God. What is it about you that does the same?

Conclude by offering a prayer of thanksgiving for God's faithful presence in your life.

✧ Review your life's journey, noting its major junctures. You may want to draw a graph of your life, marking the ups and downs along the way. At each major juncture, whether a peak or valley, ask yourself how God was present to advise and direct you. Then ask yourself how you were faithful to God at each key juncture of your life's journey.

✧ All journeys were slow in Dominic's time. If Dominic sent a letter, he could not be sure it would even reach its destination. Modern transportation and methods of communication speed up our journeys and correspondence so more people and information rapidly enter our lives. In effect, we travel to far more places than Dominic ever could. Bring to mind places in the world where enormous human suffering is taking place, places to which you have traveled via television, radio, newspapers, telephone, or fax. Pray for the people in these lands. Converse with Jesus about how you might be called to respond to this suffering.

✧ For your prayer time today, if you take a walk or a drive, invite Jesus to be your traveling companion. As you travel, point out whatever you encounter for which you are grateful (nature, beauty, friendly people) and express your thanks to Christ. Be conscious that you've invited Christ to be your traveling companion.

✧ If you are traveling through a difficult episode in your life right now, seek direction from Christ by reflecting on these words from the Scriptures:

Jesus told his friends: "Don't let your hearts be anxious. Trust me. I am the Way, the Truth, and the Life. God has sent the Holy Spirit to be with you forever. The Spirit of truth is within you even now. Believe me, my friends, I will never leave you orphans. Just have love, and I will make my home with you." (Adapted from John 14:1,6,17–18,23)

God's Word

Sing out your joy to the Creator, good people;
for praise is fitting for loyal hearts.
Give thanks to the Creator upon the harp,
with a ten-stringed lute sing songs.
O sing a new song;
play skillfully and loudly so all may hear.
For the word of the Creator is faithful,
and all God's works are to be trusted.
The Creator loves justice and right
and fills the earth with faithful love.
May your faithful love be upon us, O God,
as we place all our hope in you.

(Psalm 33:1–5,22)

Closing prayer:

May God the Father bless us,
May God the Son heal us,
May the Holy Spirit enlighten us and give us eyes to see
    with,
  ears to hear with,
  and hands to do the work of God with,
  feet to walk with,
  and a mouth to preach the word of salvation with,
  and the angel of peace to watch over us and lead us
    at last,
  by our Lord's gift, to the kingdom.

Amen.

(Tugwell, *Early Dominicans*, p. 153)

✧   **Meditation 7**   ✧

Liturgy,
the Community at Prayer

Theme: Liturgy is the prayer of the Christian church, when the community listens to the formative word of God and then celebrates its commitment to live according to that word. Dominic rooted his followers in the liturgical spirituality of the Christian church.

Opening prayer: God of all creation, you have made us your people through the waters of baptism, and you nourish us faithfully through your presence among us in word, sacrament, and one another. Help us, your chosen people, to remain ever faithful to you and to one another as we collaborate in promoting your Reign on earth.

About Dominic

The purpose of Dominic's foundation of the Order of Preachers was the preaching of the Gospel. Study was essential for effective preaching, and so was prayer. Dominic knew from personal experience that the communal, liturgical prayer of the church was essential for his preachers:

> Dominic showed in his personal life the extent to which he had absorbed and enfleshed [the church's liturgical]

tradition, while further enriching it with his own particular charism. Witnesses testify that he wished to celebrate a sung Mass every day, even while traveling on foot from place to place; that he celebrated the whole of the Office every day, together with his brethren; that he usually spent the entire night in church praying; that he spoke only with God in prayer or about God to others. To these activities he brought all the passionate intensity of one aflame with God's love, all the impatient energy of one who could not rest until the world was converted to Christ. . . . During the Eucharist, the intensity of his devotion frequently moved him to tears. (Mary Catherine Wolfe, ed., *One Mind and Heart in God: Dominican Monastic Life*, pp. 108–109)

Pause: Ask yourself, How does praying with others help me experience God?

Dominic's Words

Life was not easy for the earliest followers of Dominic. They traveled by foot, often with insufficient lodging and food. Dominic insisted on ardent study, and to all of this, he added the obligation of full monastic liturgical observance.

Yet Dominic instigated the extraordinary principle of dispensation for members of his religious order. If study or preaching responsibilities necessitated it, one could be dispensed from liturgy. Nonetheless, Dominic believed that when the community assembled for liturgy, the group prayer should be vibrant and animated. One particular anecdote has been recorded: "While the community was chanting the Office, he 'would walk around each side of the choir, exhorting and encouraging (the brethren) to sing devoutly and on key.' 'Strongly,' he would cry, 'like strong men! Sing praise to our King, but sing wisely and well'" (Wolfe, *One Mind and Heart in God*, p. 109).

Reflection

Dominic devoted himself to liturgical prayer even though he and his friars were mendicants who roamed the countryside preaching. Given the wandering life of his friars, Dominic might well have deleted some of the monastic liturgical practices typical of his era, but he did not. He believed that promoters of the Gospel must listen attentively to the word of God spoken during the various liturgical events of the day. Likewise, it was imperative that brother-preachers receive nourishment from the celebrative and communal dimensions of worship as they prepared for missionary endeavors. After all, he knew the call to Christian life was an invitation to become a member of the community of Christ's believers—the church. During communal liturgies, individual believers, giving witness of their own faith, in turn, support the faith of the other members of the community.

Baptism establishes a Christian's membership in the community, and group worship lays the foundation of the community's life. Through the Eucharist, the celebration of the other sacraments, and the Liturgy of the Hours, God's people engage in praise of God, who is the source of grace and unity. While private prayer is indispensable to the individual Christian, liturgical prayer is indispensable to the life of the believing community. In liturgy, God's word and the preaching instruct the community to the life to which it should aspire. During the Eucharist, members share the body and blood of Christ—true nourishment essential for the spiritual journey.

✧ Meditate on these Gospel words and the questions following them: "'In truth I tell you once again, if two of you on earth agree to ask anything at all, it will be granted to you by [God] in heaven. For where two or three meet in my name, I am there among them'" (Matthew 18:19–20).

✦ How is your awareness of God's presence heightened when you worship with other people?
✦ Why did Christ encourage his listeners to approach God in the company of others?
✦ Can you recall an experience of Christ's presence in a group event? What was it like?

Offer a prayer of thanksgiving for the various ways in which others have aided your communication with God.

✧ What are the needs of the people in your life? How do your loved ones, your associates, your neighbors, your town, our world, need God's assistance? As a member of the community of people that experiences these needs, make a petition to God, using the word *we* to include yourself in each request.

✧ Reflect on the last time you participated in communal worship. What was said or done at this liturgy that you found insightful or helpful? Reflect on these gifts and try to apply them to yourself.

✧ The Holy Spirit made a promise to a devout old man named Simeon that he would lay eyes on the Messiah before his death. When Mary and Joseph presented the child Jesus at the Temple, Simeon identified the child and cried out:

"Now, [God], you are letting your servant go in peace
as you promised;
for my eyes have seen the salvation
which you have made ready in the sight of the nations;
a light of revelation for the gentiles
and glory for your people Israel."

(Luke 2:29–32)

Every night in the church's liturgical Night Prayer, Simeon's words are repeated. At night, join Christians the world over by ending your day with this portion of the liturgy, Simeon's prayer. Then spend some time reflecting on and thanking God for how you experienced God's promise of salvation and goodness during the day.

✧ Read the portion of the First Letter from Paul to Timothy that appears in the "God's Word" section of this meditation. In what ways do you respond to and cooperate with the instructions given in this reading?

✧ The next time you attend liturgy, arrive early. As the worship space fills with people, recall that Christ promises to be present wherever two or more are gathered in his name. Look at people as they enter, and thank God for each one's presence with you. As the liturgy unfolds, acknowledge other ways you perceive God's presence there.

God's Word

I urge then, first of all that petitions, prayers, intercessions and thanksgiving should be offered for everyone, for [people] in authority, so that we may be able to live peaceful and quiet lives with all devotion and propriety. To do this is right, and acceptable to God our Saviour: he wants everyone to be saved and reach full knowledge of the truth. For there is only one God, and there is only one mediator between God and humanity, himself a human being, Christ Jesus, who offered himself as a ransom for all. (1 Timothy 2:1–5)

Closing prayer: Jesus, you are present to us in word, and you give us your body and blood in the Eucharist as a sign that even now we share your life. May we come to possess it completely in the realm where you live forever and ever. Amen. (Adapted from *The Roman Missal*, Prayer after Communion for the Feast of Corpus Christi, p. 349.)

✧　**Meditation 8**　✧

Christ Crucified

Theme: Dominic took to heart Paul's teaching to the Corinthians that we preach Christ crucified. He understood that only those who enjoy intimacy with Christ are capable of imparting his word to others. Consequently, Dominic spent his life developing intimacy with Christ crucified.

Opening prayer: Christ Jesus, crucified savior and friend, help me to grow in intimacy with you so that I may mirror your Gospel values in the daily movement of my life.

About Dominic

Symbols helped Dominic in his prayer. At times he would worship before the altar; other times he would pray before the image of the mother of Jesus. Frequently, Dominic contemplated the crucifix, the symbol of Christ sacrificed on the cross. One of his biographers commented, "It becomes noticeable how the crucifix came to be his central means of stirring his devotion and love of God" (Jarrett, *Life*, p. 107).

Typically, Dominic would stand before a crucifix and gaze upon it lovingly and intently. Sometimes, he would venerate Christ by bowing or genuflecting before the crucifix, offering prayers of intercession to Jesus. A favorite utterance at these times was as follows:

To you, Yahweh, I call;
my Rock, hear me.
If you do not listen,
I shall become like those who are dead.

(Psalm 28:1)

In the crucified Christ, Dominic found the mercy and compassion that nourished his spirit and served as the focal point for the preaching of the Gospel.

Pause: How would you describe your relationship with Christ crucified?

Dominic's Words

Dominic was so inflamed with love for the crucified Christ that he endeavored to imitate Christ as completely as possible. This account given by one of the friars describes Dominic's attempt to pray in union with Christ crucified:

> Sometimes, as I was told personally by someone who had seen it, our holy father Dominic was also seen praying with his hands and arms spread out like a cross, stretching himself to the limit and standing as upright as he possibly could. . . .
>
> And this was how the Lord prayed when he hung on the cross, his hands and arms stretched out, when, with great cries and weeping, his prayer was heard because of his reverence.
>
> The holy man of God, Dominic, did not use this kind of prayer regularly, but only when, by God's inspiration, he knew that some great wonder was going to occur by virtue of his prayer. He neither forbade the brethren to pray like this nor did he encourage it. . . .
>
> [Dominic would] sometimes recite, seriously, deliberately and carefully, the texts from the Psalms which refer to this manner of praying: "I cried to you, Lord, all day long I have stretched out my hands to you" (Ps. 87:10) and "I have stretched out my hands to you, my soul is like soil without water before you, speedily hear me, Lord" (Ps. 142:6–7).

This makes it possible for any devout man of prayer to understand the teaching of this father, praying in this way when he desired to be extraordinarily moved towards God by the power of his prayer. (Tugwell, *Early Dominicans*, pp. 98–99)

Reflection

Once Dominic accepted his role as a partner with the crucified Savior in spreading the news of Christ's death and resurrection, he studied and prayed to nurture his loving relationship with him. The crucified Christ gave to Dominic and gives to us the perfect model for complete love.

When gymnasts wish to reproduce a champion's daring maneuver or sculptors want to imitate a master artist's technique, they study their mentor carefully, noticing each nuance or action. In their imagination, they re-enact exactly what their mentor did, over and over again. By focusing all of their attention on their mentor, gymnasts or sculptors hope to become more like them, even while maintaining their uniqueness.

By analogy, when Dominic or we contemplate the crucified Christ, we identify with him, hoping to learn fidelity, courage, the desire to do God's will, and the great love of one willing to give up life for others. As Jesus gave his flesh to the eternal God, all Christians are called to be the Body of Christ today.

✧ Place yourself in the presence of a crucifix. Ponder the depths of love that Christ has for you.

✧ Meditatively read the story of Christ's crucifixion and resurrection in Mark, chapters 15 and 16. Then meditate on this question: What do these events have to do with my life today?

✧ What follows is a guided meditation about the presence of Jesus in your life. In preparation, you may want to review the suggestions for using guided meditation, given in the foreword.

In the presence of your Holy Friend, relax your whole body, starting with your feet and finishing with your head. . . . Breathe deeply and slowly, welcoming the breath of life and the Spirit of God. . . . Remember or imagine the most beautiful place in nature, a place in which you feel blessed and totally peaceful. . . . Rest in this scene. . . . Breathe deeply, relaxing in the beauty of the moment. . . .

In the distance, you see Jesus walking toward you. . . . As he comes closer, you see that his eyes are merry, and he is smiling. . . . You prepare to meet him. . . . He stands before you and stretches out his arms to embrace you. . . . Hesitating for just a moment, you reach out your arms in response and embrace him. . . . After some moments, the two of you sit down together. . . .

Jesus looks into your eyes and says, "Tell me what is on your mind and in your heart, my friend." . . . After collecting your emotions and thoughts, you begin talking with him. . . . As he speaks, you listen carefully. . . .

When your conversation ends, Jesus stands to go. . . . He hugs you once again, saying, "Peace be with you." . . . You gaze upon him as he walks away. . . .

When you are ready, open your eyes. Many people find it helpful to write down their reactions to guided meditations in a journal.

✧ Different names for Jesus represent certain ways of being in relationship with him. For example, the name *Prince of Peace* connotes a much different image than does *Good Shepherd* or *Gentle Companion*. List all of the names that you associate with Jesus, and then choose your own favorite name for Christ, the one that best touches your experience of him right now. Repeatedly pray this name slowly and meditatively.

✧ Pray a litany to Christ, using as many different names or titles for him as you can. After each title, pray "have mercy on me." Reflect on the meaning that each title has in your life. To help you begin, several titles are provided here. After praying with these titles, continue the litany with your own names for Jesus.

Christ, have mercy on me.
Lord, have mercy on me.
Jesus, Word of God, have mercy on me.
Gentle Friend, have mercy on me.
Faithful Companion, have mercy on me.
Sacred Heart of Jesus, have mercy on me.
Son of God and Son of Mary, have mercy on me.

✧ Read the portion of the First Letter from Paul to the Corinthians provided in the "God's Word" section of this meditation. Reflect on the ways your life manifests to others the events described in this reading.

God's Word

The tradition I handed on to you in the first place, a tradition which I had myself received, was that Christ died for our sins, in accordance with the scriptures, and that he was buried; and that on the third day, he was raised to life, in accordance with the scriptures; and that he appeared to Cephas; and later to the Twelve. (1 Corinthians 15:3–5)

Closing prayer:

O Holy One,
send down your abundant blessing
upon your people who have devoutly recalled the
     death of your Son
in the sure hope of the resurrection.
Grant them pardon; bring them comfort.
May their faith grow stronger
and their eternal salvation be assured.
(Adapted from The Roman Missal,
Prayer over the people for Good Friday, p. 167)

Mary,
Model of Discipleship

Theme: Dominican tradition has always looked to Mary, the mother of Jesus, as the perfect model for Christian discipleship.

Opening prayer: Hail Mary, full of grace! The Lord is with you. Blessed are you among women, and blessed is the fruit of your womb, Jesus.

About Dominic

Dominic assembled his followers and urged them, by means of a lengthy and eloquent sermon, to love and reverence the mother of Jesus always. During his periods of prayer, he was known to have stayed for long hours before the shrine of the mother of Jesus, offering her homage and learning from her own example as a disciple of her Son.

Although there is no clear proof that the devotion to the rosary actually began with Dominic, tradition holds that during a supernatural experience, Mary gave him the task of introducing and promulgating the devotion to the rosary. The rosary is not prayed to worship Mary, but rather it is intended to help those praying reflect on the various episodes of

Christ's life in company with Mary. One explanation of why tradition links Dominic to the rosary comes from his own style of prayer:

> His own way of prayer, consisting, as we have seen, of vocal expressions of love and adoration, was intermingled with silences; it passed from speech to contemplation as it fixed itself on to the character of our Lord. All these elements were united in the rosary. It was contemplative and vocal. . . .
>
> . . . The mere recitation of prayers would be no use unless these could be accompanied by a consciousness of God's presence. . . . Hence it was necessary to add the idea of some sort of mystery, some act or scene of our Lord's life, and present it vividly to the imagination so as ultimately to stir the heart to love and worship. . . . The recitation became almost a mechanical aid to reflection. . . . The purpose of the rosary was, therefore, to produce the effect that St Dominic had in view in all his prayers, an intense application of the human soul to the divine personality of Christ. (Jarrett, *Life*, pp. 110–111)

Dominican tradition suggests that Dominic exhorted his listeners to manifest Christ's life, which is outlined in the fifteen mysteries of the rosary, in their own daily life. Mary would be their advocate with her Son.

Pause: Ponder this question: How is Mary an inspiration to you as you face the challenges of living as a disciple of Christ?

Dominic's Words

According to tradition, Dominic told this story to a Dominican nun named Sister Cecilia:

> One night . . . as [Dominic] stood praying, he glanced at the other end of the dormitory and saw three . . . women enter. He noticed that the one in the middle was a venerable lady of greater beauty and dignity than the

other two. One of the two was carrying a beautiful, shining vessel and the other a [holy water sprinkler] which she handed to the lady in the center. This lady sprinkled the brethren and blessed them. She said to Blessed Dominic: "I am the one you call upon each evening. When you say, 'Turn then most gracious advocate,' I prostrate myself before my Son and ask him to preserve this Order."

. . . [Afterwards, Dominic] was caught up in spirit before God and saw the Lord and the Blessed Virgin sitting at his right. . . .

As Blessed Dominic looked around, he could see religious of all the orders but his own before the throne of God. He began to weep bitterly and stood apart, not daring to approach the Lord and his Mother. Then Our Lady motioned for him to come near. But he would not dare, until the Lord himself also called him.

Blessed Dominic cast himself down before them weeping bitterly. The Lord told him to rise, and when he did, asked him, "Why are you weeping so?" "I am weeping because I see all the other orders here but no sign of my own." The Lord said to him, "Do you want to see your Order?" and he answered, "Yes, Lord." Then the Blessed Virgin opened the cloak she was wearing and spread it out before Blessed Dominic, to whom it seemed vast enough to cover the entire heaven, and under it he saw a large multitude of the brethren.

. . . After that the vision disappeared. (*Supplement to the Liturgy of the Hours for the Order of Preachers*, pp. 131–132)

Reflection

Since the earliest centuries of Christianity, devotion to Mary has been present in Christian spirituality in a variety of forms. At times these devotions strayed from their initial intent. At its best, Marian devotion has meant turning to Mary, the first disciple of Jesus, and following her instructions to the stewards at the wedding feast of Cana, "'Do whatever he tells you'" (John 2:5).

Throughout his life, Dominic's devotion to Mary supported and inspired his preaching. Like Dominic, all Christians are called to do precisely what Mary did—live and perpetuate the Gospel way of life, which has been given to us by Jesus of Nazareth. Mary can serve as our support and inspiration too.

✧ Pray one or all the decades of the rosary. If you have seldom or never prayed the rosary, here are directions:
1. Begin at the crucifix by making the sign of the cross and praying the Apostles' Creed.
2. At the first bead, pray the Lord's Prayer.
3. Pray a Hail Mary for each of the next three beads.
4. At the next bead, pray the Glory Be to the Father.
5. Start the first decade (the first grouping of ten beads) by taking a moment or two to recall one of the mysteries listed below for reflection and then praying the Lord's Prayer.
6. Pray ten Hail Marys, one for each bead.
7. Finish the decade with the Glory Be to the Father.
8. Repeat steps 5, 6, and 7 for each of the remaining four decades.

The fifteen mysteries for meditation are listed below. As you pray each decade, ponder the sacred event, asking yourself how the mystery or event you are recalling tells your own life story. Of course, each mystery can also be a complete meditation exercise in itself, without the need of praying the rosary beads along with it.

The Joyful Mysteries
1. *The annunciation of the birth of Jesus (Luke 1:26–38):* How do you receive Christ into your innermost being and nourish that sacred presence?
2. *The visitation of Elizabeth by Mary (Luke 1:39–56):* How does the life of Christ within you impel you to reach out and care for others just as Mary went to care for her cousin Elizabeth?
3. *The nativity of Jesus (Luke 2:1–20):* How do you make Christ more present in the world through your attitudes, actions, words, projects?
4. *The presentation in the Temple (Luke 2:22–38):* How integral to your life is offering thanksgiving to God for the gifts you have enjoyed?
5. *The finding of the lost child (Luke 2:41–50):* In what ways do you share your gifts, resources, and knowledge?

The Sorrowful Mysteries
6. *The agony in the garden (Luke 22:39–46):* When you are challenged and in pain, how is God a source of strength and support to you?
7. *The scourging of Jesus (Mark 15:15):* How can you purify yourself of habits and practices that are not helpful to your growth in wholeness and holiness?
8. *The crowning with thorns (Mark 15:16–20):* Jesus' persecutors performed the ultimate indignity by ridiculing his kingship. How do you insist upon and protect the dignity of others in society?
9. *The carrying of the cross (Luke 23:26–31):* Even in this inhumane experience, Jesus continued to care for those he encountered. How does Christ call you to be available to needy people?
10. *The Crucifixion (Luke 23:32–49):* In what ways is your life a complete offering to God? Are there ways in which you can become more completely turned over to God?

The Glorious Mysteries

11. *The Resurrection (John 20:1–18):* Mary of Magdala was the first person commissioned by Christ to tell others about his resurrection. What does it mean to be called by name by Jesus? In what ways do you share the Christian faith with others?

12. *The ascension of Jesus (Acts 1:3–9):* Is Christ central in your life? Reflect on how your life is a journey toward oneness with God.

13. *The descent of the Holy Spirit (Acts 2:1–4):* The Holy Spirit became manifest to the assembled disciples. Where is your fire of the Holy Spirit? How does your relationship with other Christians enhance your faith life?

14. *The assumption of Mary into heaven (Song of Songs 2:8–14):* As Mary dwells in the presence of God in eternity, ponder what it means to live in the presence of God in this life.

15. *The crowning of Mary as queen of heaven and earth (Revelation 12:1–6):* As this mystery turns our thoughts to the Reign of God, examine how active you are in promoting the Reign of God among people in this life.

✧ "Mary said, 'You see before you the Lord's servant, let it happen to me as you have said.' And the angel left her" (Luke 1:38).

✦ Read this short quotation slowly and prayerfully.

✦ How do you serve the interests of God in your everyday life?

✦ Among your friends and acquaintances, whom would you consider to be a servant of the Lord? What qualities make them so? Do you feel drawn to emulating these qualities?

✧ Turn to the "God's Word" section of this meditation and read Mary's canticle, also known as the Magnificat. After reading the canticle, return to these questions:

✦ Mary's opening words, "My being proclaims your greatness," announce that through her humanity, the eternal Word of God is brought forth in human form in time and space. How is God's goodness and greatness brought forth in the world through you?

✦ When Mary acknowledged that "all ages to come shall call me blessed," she knew that what she did in her lifetime would make a difference in the world. How does your life make a difference in the world? How is this world a better place in which to live because of you?

✧ Reconsider Mary's words at Cana, "'Do whatever he tells you'" (John 2:5). How have you been cooperative with that instruction today?

God's Word

Mary responded to God's call in the Magnificat:

My being proclaims your greatness,
and my spirit finds joy in you, God my Savior.

For you have looked upon me, your servant, in my
    lowliness;
all ages to come shall call me blessed.

God, you who are mighty, have done great things for me.
Holy is your name.

Your mercy is from age to age toward those who fear you.

You have shown might with your arm
and confused the proud in their inmost thoughts.

You have deposed the mighty from their thrones
and raised the lowly to high places.

The hungry you have given every good thing
while the rich you have sent away empty.

You have upheld Israel your servant, ever mindful of
    your mercy—

even as you promised our ancestors;
promised Abraham, Sarah, and their descendants forever.
                    (Nancy Schreck and Maureen Leach, comps.,
                        Psalms Anew: In Inclusive Language, p. 16)

Closing prayer:

Mother of the liberator, pray for us.
Mother of the homeless, pray for us.
Mother of the dying, pray for us.
Mother of the nonviolent, pray for us.
Widowed mother, pray for us.
Unwed mother, pray for us.
Mother of a political prisoner, pray for us.
Mother of the condemned, pray for us.
Mother of the executed criminal, pray for us.
Woman of mercy, empower us.
Woman of faith, empower us.
Woman of contemplation, empower us.
Woman of vision, empower us.
Woman of wisdom, empower us.
Woman of grace and truth, empower us.
Woman, pregnant with hope, empower us.
Woman, centered in God, empower us.

(Condensed from the "Litany of Mary of Nazareth"
distributed for the Marian Year 1987–88
by Pax Christi USA)

Trust

Theme: Through his teaching and example, Dominic exhorted his followers to accept Christ's invitation to completely trust the all-provident God.

Opening prayer: O Divine Providence, help me to trust your presence and love in my life. Heal my lack of trust, so that I may live in peace and contentment in your care always.

About Dominic

The mendicant friars had to depend on God's providence each day. Dominic sometimes stretched the limits of his brothers' trust in him and in God. At times, people regarded the depth of Dominic's trust in God to be foolhardy.

The Bull of Approval for the foundation of the preaching community was issued at Rome on 22 December 1216. One day later, a more significant document, the Bull of Confirmation of the Order was issued. In subsequent months, other official documents were promulgated that further defined and clarified the lifestyle and mission of the fledgling community.

During the next summer, Dominic assembled the band of preachers, ostensibly to provide further formation for the brethren and to give them an opportunity to grow and bond as a community.

To everyone's astonishment, on 15 August 1216, Dominic announced, "'hoarded grain goes bad,'" and accordingly, he sent four preachers to Spain; seven to Paris; two to Prouille to serve the nuns there; and one companion accompanied Dominic to Rome (Tugwell, *Early Dominicans*, p. 16). Even as these events were in process, four more recruits entered the ranks of the preachers.

The brothers of the community were astounded; some of the clergy and hierarchy were incredulous; still others disapproved. They scoffed at Dominic for dispersing the preachers before they had sufficient time to become adequately prepared for their arduous task and sufficiently committed to one another.

Nonetheless, Dominic trusted in the providence of God, whose work he was furthering; and in the spirit of that trust, he introduced the order to its international mission—a mission that proved quite successful. By the time of Dominic's death five years later (6 August 1221), about three hundred preaching friars were distributed throughout France, Italy, Spain, Germany, Scandinavia, Hungary, Poland, and England. Correspondingly, at the time of Dominic's death, women of the order occupied monasteries in Spain, France, and Italy.

Pause: Do you really trust that God will always be present to you, no matter how trying the circumstances may become?

Dominic's Words

Another legend about Dominic portrays his reliance on God's beneficence:

> [Dominic] returned to Italy in company with a . . . brother named John. This brother became so reduced from hunger in the Lombard Alps that he could not move a step further, nor even rise to his feet. "What ails you, my son?" enquired the gentle father. "Why do you not keep up with me!" "Father, I am truly dying of hunger," cried the weary brother. "Take courage then, my son, let

us go just a little further and we shall get all we want for recruiting our strength." But as the brother still held out, avowing he could not drag himself a step farther, the saint, with that kindness and sweet pity for which he was ever remarkable, had recourse to his usual refuge of fervent prayer. For a brief space he communed with God, and then addressed the brother once more: "Rise up, son, go straight before you to yonder spot, and bring back what you find there." The brother got up with difficulty, and dragging himself to the spot indicated—which was about a stone's throw off—saw there an exceedingly white loaf wrapt in a snow-white cloth, which he brought back with him; then after eating until his strength revived he continued his journey.

Now when they had gone some way on, the brother began to think the matter over, and in his amazement cried out: "My God, who put the bread in that lonely spot? Where can it have come from? Surely I must have parted with my wits not to have made further enquiries about it?" Then addressing St Dominic he said: "Father, where did yon bread come from? Whoever put it there?" Upon which [Dominic] rejoined: "My son, have you not had as much as you wanted?" "Yes, father," said the other. "Very well then, since you have had as much as pleased you, thank God for it, and trouble yourself no more about it." (Conway and Jarrett, *Lives of the Brethren*, pp. 47–48)

Reflection

Dominic believed quite literally that God would provide. When he roamed the countryside and town streets preaching, he had one set of clothes, and depended on the generosity of the people from whom he begged. While not all of us are called upon to live in exactly the same way, Dominic's reliance on God's providence offers an example for all of us to follow in trusting our God of love.

Christ loves us as he loved Dominic. His love is uncondi-
tional, always forgiving, and generous. He assures us in the
Scriptures that we only need ask for anything in God's name,
and it will be granted to us. This reliance frees us from anxiety, as it freed Dominic, and invites us to praise and thank
God.

✧ Slowly pray the Lord's Prayer. Then return to the
phrase, "Give us this day our daily bread." Ponder the meaning of that expression of trust in your life.

✧ God cares for all people, often through the care and
concern of others. Make a list of the people who show you
God's providence by their care for you; thank God for each
person. Then, list and thank God for all the people to whom
you manifest God's providential care.

✧ Whom do you know whose life is clearly rooted in
trust in God's providence? How can the example of this person help you to grow in total reliance upon God?

✧ Ponder this entry from the diary of Anne Frank. During the many months that her family hid from the Nazis,
cooped in an attic in Amsterdam, Anne registered her most
poignant thoughts. In the face of so much fear, she found comfort in God's care. She wrote:

> In the evening, when I lie in bed and end my prayers with
> the words, "I thank you, God, for all that is good and
> dear and beautiful," I am filled with joy. Then I think
> about "the good" of going into hiding, of my health and
> with my whole being of the "dearness" of Peter . . . and
> of "the beauty" which exists in the world. . . .
> I don't think then of all the misery, but of the beauty
> that still remains. . . .
> . . . Look at these things, then you find yourself
> again, and God, and then you regain your balance. (B. M.
> Mooyaart-Doubleday, trans., *Anne Frank: The Diary of a
> Young Girl*, p. 184)

Now, recall a time of suffering from your distant past. Are there ways in which you have grown as a result of that suffering? For example, are you more compassionate or understanding today because of this painful episode you are recalling? What "beauty" did God send you through this suffering? Do you trust God more now?

Offer thanksgiving for the richness you have derived from this difficult experience in your life, recalling that God's ways of providing for our good are not always the expected ways.

✧ Imagine that Jesus is speaking directly to you using the words in the "God's Word" section. Read the words slowly several times. Then converse with Jesus about the meaning of the words for you.

God's Word

"I am telling you not to worry about your life and what you are to eat, nor about your body and what you are to wear. Surely life is more than food, and the body more than clothing! Look at the birds in the sky. They do not sow or reap or gather into barns; yet your [Creator] feeds them. Are you not worth much more than they are? Can any of you, however much you worry, add one single cubit to your span of life? And why worry about clothing? Think of the flowers growing in the fields; they never have to work or spin; yet I assure you that not even Solomon in all his royal robes was clothed like one of these. . . . Set your hearts on [God's Reign] first, and on God's saving justice, and all these other things will be given you as well." (Matthew 6:25–33)

Closing prayer: God of trust, letting go of the concerns of the day and placing my trust completely in you is not easy to do. Day by day increase my confidence in your holy providence, so that I can praise you in the same carefree manner as the lilies of the field and the birds of the air.

✧ Meditation 11 ✧

Humility

Theme: Humility means living with the truth. Whatever we have comes from God's goodness—that is a central truth. Appreciating this fact, Dominic praised and thanked God. He also focused his efforts on doing God's will instead of fretting about his status or other people's opinion of him.

Opening prayer: Holy One, giver of all gifts, show me the path to true humility. I know that whatever I have comes from your love. Help me to understand this better. I praise and thank you for your goodness and beg the grace to do your will.

About Dominic

Dominic's attitude toward his position of leadership within the preaching order evidenced his humility. About five years after the papal recognition, Dominic gathered the membership together for a legislative assembly that has come to be called a "chapter" in the order's tradition.

First, Dominic stipulated that the convened chapter rank as the highest unit of government within the order. Dominic himself was subject to the authority of the chapter—a revolutionary initiative in religious life for that time. In most communities, the abbot or superior held extensive powers and served for life. To this day, Dominican chapters are held regularly, and those serving leadership terms join the ranks of the chapter membership as equals throughout the chapter process.

At the first chapter meeting, an even more astonishing event occurred—Dominic resigned as superior. Seeing that the preaching work was progressing well and that his physical strength was waning, he recognized the truth. He did not have the energy to continue leading the friars and knew he was not indispensable. So he announced to the shocked chapter, "'I deserve to be removed from office, as I am unfit for the post and remiss'" (Hinnebusch, *The Dominicans*, p. 13).

Quite predictably, the assembly steadfastly refused to accept Dominic's resignation, and he continued in his office until his death the year following the order's historic first chapter meeting.

Pause: Ponder this question: Am I able to face the hard truths about myself?

Dominic's Words

Dominic's humility compelled him to pray earnestly for whatever graces he believed he needed to do his ministry. Indeed, the first of the nine ways of Dominic's prayer outlines how people should seek God's will and ask for what is needed:

> Bowing humbly before the altar . . . he used sometimes to say to the brethren the text from Judith, "The prayer of the humble and meek has always been pleasing to you." It was by humility that the Canaanite woman obtained what she wanted, and so did the prodigal son. Also, "I am not worthy to have you come under my roof." "Lord, humble my spirit deeply because, Lord, I am utterly humbled before you." So [Dominic], standing with his body erect, would bow his head and his heart humbly before Christ his Head, considering his own servile condition and the outstanding nobility of Christ, and giving himself up entirely to venerating Him. (Tugwell, *Early Dominicans*, p. 95)

Recognizing that all gifts come from God, Dominic could encourage and support the friars when they felt inadequate in their task of preaching. In this story, Dominic helps one of his brothers realize the truth:

> Through June and July [Dominic] stayed in Paris, dispersing his brethren to Limoges, Rheims, Metz, Poitiers, Orleans, stimulating their studies and particularly encouraging his earlier companions, who were rather out of their element among this newer set of graduates and professors. Peter Seila [Peter Selhan], at first the mainstay of the Order, was rather frightened to find himself, a merchant, among all these intellectual recruits. . . . Peter consulted Dominic, who replied: "Go, my son, go in all confidence. Twice a day you shall be with me in my prayers. Do not fail me, for you will win many souls and be of much profit." The saint's fire re-enkindled the zeal of Peter, and the prophecy came true. (Jarrett, *Life*, pp. 90–91)

Dominic stressed the academic preparation of his friars, but he knew that in truth, God's grace was the essential element that made them effective preachers. Under Dominic's tutelage, Peter Selhan came to see this same truth and became more humble as a result.

Reflection

Humility—recognition and acceptance of the truth that all gifts come from God—challenges us to become comfortable with our gifts and mindful of our rough edges. Humility urges us to acknowledge our skills, talents, beauty, and life as gifts, and to accept any affirmation or appreciation of these things when it is rendered. All of our attributes and abilities are God's gifts.

And how does the humble person respond to God's bounty? Dominic praised and thanked God in prayer. He also regularly prayed for what he needed. Finally, recognizing the crying needs of other people, Dominic, like Jesus, gave us the example of humble self-giving. Following Dominic's example, we should be mindful that all gifts should be shared because all humankind is the Body of Christ.

✧ Examine your response to God's gifts to you. Meditate on these questions:

✦ Am I able to accept compliments and affirmation?
✦ How do I respond when I am being praised? Why?
✦ How can I continue to grow in my ability to react humbly—that is, truthfully—to affirmation and praise?

✧ Humility calls us to an honest examination of God's truth that is present in our everyday life. Converse with God about these questions:

✦ Are you frequently tired? Are you listening to your body's demands for proper rest, nourishment, and exercise?
✦ Are you lonely? If so, can this be a message that you have not been spending quality time with people for whom you care?
✦ Do other people find you irritable? To what wholesome human needs might you be insufficiently attentive?

Ask God to help you be responsive to the messages in your life that require humble listening.

✧ Pray with this passage from Paul's Letter to the Philippians:

Make your own the mind of Christ Jesus:

Who, being in the form of God,
did not count equality with God
something to be grasped.

But he emptied himself,
taking the form of a slave,
becoming as human beings are;

and being in every way like a human being,
he was humbler yet,
even to accepting death, death on a cross.

(2:5–8)

How are you putting on the mind of Jesus, taking on the form of a servant to your sisters and brothers? Do you ever find yourself grasping for control? Talk with Jesus about both of these questions.

✧ Throughout your life, who have been the people who have taught you the most about goodness, love, and justice?
+ Reflect on the qualities you have learned from your "mentors."
+ How are you faithful to these teachers of life's lessons?
+ How do you pass these lessons on to other people?
+ Thank God for your mentors and for your responses to them.

✧ Pray slowly and repeatedly these words: "The prayer of the humble and meek has always been pleasing to you." Then open your heart to God, asking for the gifts that you need.

✧ Dominic sang in God's honor. In recognition that God is the giver of all goodness, sing or hum "Amazing Grace" or another hymn that acknowledges God's bounty.

God's Word

Then Jesus appeared: he came from Galilee to the Jordan to be baptised by John. John tried to dissuade him, with the words, "It is I who need baptism from you, and yet you come to me!" But Jesus replied, "Leave it like this for the time being; it is fitting that we should, in this way, do all that uprightness demands." (Matthew 3:13–15)

Closing prayer:

The world and all that is in it belong to Yahweh,
the earth and all who live on it.
Yahweh built it on the deep waters,
laid its foundations in the oceans' depths.
Who has the right to climb Yahweh's mountain?

Or stand in this holy place?
Those who are pure in act and in thought,
who do not worship idols
or make false promises.
Yahweh will bless them.
God their Savior will give them salvation.
Such are the people who come to God.

(Psalm 24:1–6)

Freedom

Theme: Jesus calls us to love our neighbors as ourselves and to love God. God wills for us to be fully alive. But, our Creator grants us free will because love cannot be forced. Dominic wanted his followers to obey God's will to love, but recognized that they had to choose to do so freely. He trusted that God's grace would protect them from evil ways.

Opening prayer: Loving God, I treasure the gift of free will with which you have blessed humanity. With that gift, I want to grow in my desire to do your will. May I freely choose to love you, your people, and all of your creation.

About Dominic

Many religious communities of Dominic's time legislated to the smallest detail as to how their members should conduct themselves. These were the days of monarchies; freedom was suspect. Yet Dominic's style of leadership encouraged his followers to choose Christ freely. As a result, many religious, clerics, and nobility criticized Dominic for letting his preachers have so much latitude in their travels, schedule, and other facets of life:

> [Dominic] used to travel round and send out his first brethren, even though he had only a few and they were

indifferently educated and mostly young. Some religious of the Cistercian Order were amazed at this, and particularly at the confident way he sent such young friars out to preach. They set themselves to watch these young men, to see if they could find fault with anything they did or said. He put up with this for some time, but one day, filled with a holy boldness, he asked them, "Why do you spy on my disciples, you disciples of the Pharisees? I know, I know for certain, that my young men will go out and come back, will be sent out and will return; but your young men will be kept locked up and will still go out." (Tugwell, *Early Dominicans*, p. 91)

Indeed, Dominic's rebuff of the criticism reflected his belief that many of the monasteries, while maintaining outward appearances of virtue, were actually rife with corruption. If the Order of Preachers was to fulfill its mission, the friars would have to be free to wander, to meet all sorts of people, and sometimes to err. Dominic had Jesus' response to the Pharisees and scribes clearly in mind: "'It is not those who are well who need the doctor, but the sick. I have come to call not the upright but sinners to repentance'" (Luke 5:31–32). Preaching repentance required that the friars be free to live among sinners and to trust that God's grace would keep them from evil ways.

Pause: Reflect on how your friendship with God can bring a greater sense of freedom into your life.

Dominic's Words

Although the Primitive Constitutions for the Order of Preachers were not penned literally by Dominic, they authentically convey much of his spirit. Freedom was such an essential component of Christian life for Dominic that he legislated two unconventional principles for the preachers.

First, he decreed that his disciples would not be committing sin if they failed in the observance of their rules. This sharply contrasted with the rules of other religious communities.

Second, Dominic advocated the principle of dispensation, whereby one could be dispensed (or even presume dispensation) from important community events under certain circumstances. This excerpt from the Dominican Primitive Constitutions illustrates these liberating policies:

> However, the superior is to have the right to dispense the brethren in his own community whenever it seems useful to him, particularly in things which seem likely to obstruct study or preaching or the good of souls, since our Order is known to have been founded initially precisely for the sake of preaching and the salvation of souls, and all our concern should be primarily and passionately directed to this all-important goal, that we should be able to be useful to the souls of our neighbours. Priors are to use dispensations just like all the other brethren.
>
> Therefore, to provide for the unity and peace of the whole Order, we intend and declare that our Constitutions do not bind us on pain of sin, but only on pain of a penance. . . . And we have carefully compiled this book, which we name the Book of Customs. (Tugwell, *Early Dominicans*, p. 457)

Reflection

Christ's Gospel is replete with directives: be loving, be just, be honest, be forgiving, be faithful, be compassionate. If people do behave according to the Gospel mandates, the world will actually become more loving, just, honest, reconciled, faithful, and compassionate. In other words, to the extent that men and women observe Christ's commands, life becomes more free of the causes of pain and distress. Christ is all truth; the truth makes us free. Putting on Christ is the freest form of living.

Distance from sin results in freedom from fear, anxiety, and all other forms of internal imprisonment. The Gospel mandates, which Dominic spent a lifetime preaching and integrating into his own life, generate for oneself and for others this holy freedom. As Jesus did, Dominic invites us to enter freely into a relationship with Christ.

✧ Pray repeatedly this passage from the Gospel of John:

"If you make my word your home
you will indeed be my disciples;
you will come to know the truth,
and the truth will set you free."

(8:31–32)

Then ask Jesus to tell you what truths you need to know about yourself in order to be free. Sit quietly and listen to what the Spirit of Jesus tells you.

✧ Compose your own litany of prayers for freedom. Ask Jesus to free you from the compulsions and sins that imprison you and to free the world from its sinfulness. After each petition, pray, "Christ Jesus, Liberator, reveal the way to freedom." Here are some sample petitions, but compose your own litany.

✦ That I may let go of some of my anger toward _____,
I pray . . .
(Christ Jesus, Liberator, reveal the way to freedom.)
✦ For those whose past pains leave them unable to trust,
I pray . . .
✦ For those whose greed causes them to deprive others,
I pray . . .
✦ For those whose ignorance of the Gospel leads them to oppress others, I pray . . .

✧ Ponder the causes of pain, anxiety, war, and unhappiness in the world around you. Then page slowly through the Gospel of Matthew looking for words of Jesus that show the ways to alleviate pain, anxiety, war, and unhappiness. Ask the Holy Spirit to enlighten others and yourself with a deeper understanding of these Gospel teachings. Another time, you might want to do the same exercise using another of the Gospel accounts.

✧ Read Robert Frost's poem "The Road Not Taken," which follows, and then ponder the questions that follow it.

Two roads diverged in a yellow wood,
And sorry I could not travel both
And be one traveler, long I stood
And looked down one as far as I could
To where it bent in the undergrowth;

Then took the other, as just as fair,
And having perhaps the better claim,
Because it was grassy and wanted wear;
Though as for that the passing there
Had worn them really about the same,

And both that morning equally lay
In leaves no step had trodden black.
Oh, I kept the first for another day!
Yet knowing how way leads on to way,
I doubted if I should ever come back.

I shall be telling this with a sigh
Somewhere ages and ages hence:
Two roads diverged in a wood, and I—
I took the one less traveled by,
And that has made all the difference.

(Robert Frost, "The Road Not Taken")

✦ How is the Gospel way of life a trip down a road less traveled?

✦ What difference does the Gospel make in your everyday life?

✦ What is hard about claiming the freedom necessary to grow in your response to the Gospel or to take the road less traveled?

✦ Ask God to help you have the freedom necessary to follow the Gospel path.

✧ Read "God's Word" as it appears in this meditation and then reflect on the meaning of love in your life and how love leads you to greater freedom.

God's Word

After all, brothers [and sisters], you were called to be free; do not use your freedom as an opening for self-indulgence, but be servants to one another in love, since the whole of the Law is summarised in the one commandment: You must love your neighbour as yourself. If you go snapping at one another and tearing one another to pieces, take care: you will be eaten up by one another.

Instead, I tell you, be guided by the Spirit, and you will no longer yield to self-indulgence. The desires of self-indulgence are always in opposition to the Spirit, . . . one against the other; that is how you are prevented from doing the things that you want to. But when you are led by the Spirit, you are not under the Law. . . . The fruit of the Spirit is love, joy, peace, patience, kindness, goodness, trustfulness, gentleness and self-control; no law can touch such things as these. All who belong to Christ Jesus have crucified self with all its passions and its desires. (Galatians 5:13–24)

Closing prayer: Liberating God, help me to become free of attachment to those things that imprison my soul, mind, and body. You are truth and freedom. With your help, I yearn for a life in which I am totally free to be who you designed me to be—a loving ambassador of the freeing Good News.

Mercy and Compassion

Theme: Dominic, who always endeavored to follow the Gospel way of life, was noted for his mercy and compassion. Because of his awareness of the pain and suffering caused by sin, he constantly prayed for God's mercy for all humankind.

Opening prayer: O God, be merciful to me, a sinner. May your mercy shower upon me, so that I may, in turn, show mercy and compassion to other people.

About Dominic

Dominic showed deep compassion for those who found themselves in trouble or in need, either physically or spiritually. One story illustrates the depths of Dominic's mercy and compassion for other people.

At one point, probably in the course of a battle at Alarcos, Spain, in 1195, the Moors captured a young man whose sister was an acquaintance of Dominic. Customarily, the victors sold the vanquished into slavery. Desperately seeking help for her brother, the sister begged Dominic to intervene in some way.

Moved with compassion over the plight of this man who was about to be taken into slavery to a foreign land, Dominic decided to help. Because he had no money with which to barter for the captive's release, he offered himself in exchange for the unfortunate man.

Providentially, the release was effected without Dominic's having to become a slave. Nevertheless, Dominic stood ready to become enslaved for the sake of another human being.

Pause: Ask yourself this question: Can I honestly describe myself as generally compassionate and merciful?

Dominic's Words

Sin causes untold pain and suffering; Dominic never doubted this. He felt deeply the pain people suffered due to the sins and offenses of others. Dominic felt compassion for the victims of sin and for the sinners too. Throughout his nightly prayer vigils, he would be so moved with anguish about the cruelty, violence, and hate in the world that he would sometimes cry out, asking God what was to become of sinners. He bequeathed this deep concern for human suffering to his disciples.

One of the brothers wrote,

> So wonderfully tender-hearted was he touching the sins and miseries of men, that when he came near any city or town from where he could overlook it, he would burst into tears at the thought of the miseries of mankind, of the sins committed therein, and of the numbers who were [headed for destruction]. (Conway and Jarrett, *Lives of the Brethren*, p. 56)

He exhorted the members of his community to pray with mercy and compassion as well. He would say to them,

> "If you cannot weep for your own sins, because you have none, still there are many sinners to be directed to God's mercy and love, and the prophets and apostles prayed for them with great groanings, and for their sake too Jesus wept when he saw them, and similarly the holy David, saying 'I saw the half-hearted and I pined away.'" (Tugwell, *The Nine Ways*, pp. 18–20)

Reflection

Jesus is the model of mercy and compassion. In the biblical stories, Jesus confronted people suffering or sinners with remarkable gentleness and encouragement.

When he encountered the angry mob that wanted to execute the adulterous woman, Jesus did not whitewash her sin, nor did he condemn her. Instead, he offered her mercy and compassion, inviting her to reform her life and grow in grace and dignity. When he met other sinners—Mary of Magdala, for instance—Jesus did not pretend that their sins were not destructive. He invited them to reform and become the best they could be. He met them with mercy and compassion.

With mercy and compassion, Jesus healed the woman doubled over, the paralyzed man, and blind Bartimaeus. Jesus came to make people whole spiritually, emotionally, and physically.

Like anyone who has put on the mind of Christ, Dominic learned mercy and compassion well.

✧ Relax. Pray the name *Jesus* until you have focused on his presence within you. Bring to mind your shortcomings, and after naming each one, pray aloud the litany of mercy:

Lord, have mercy.
Christ, have mercy.
Lord, have mercy.

Next, ask Jesus to help you become a more merciful and compassionate person.

✧ Dominic prayed for his sinful world. Pray for people who have recently committed crimes against humanity and the earth. Pray for reforms in society that might alleviate the conditions that drive people to crime. Talk with Jesus about your own participation in such reforms.

✧ Draw up a list of people needing healing of soul, emotions, or body. Pray for each person, asking for God's healing. If possible, reach out to these people. For instance, if someone is sick, visit him or her.

✧ Picture yourself talking comfortably with Jesus. Ask him to tell you about those areas of your life that concern him. Listen to what Jesus has to say. Listen to your own responses to Jesus. Make a personal resolution as a result of this visit with the Gentle One.

✧ Read the story of the accused woman (John 8:3–11) provided in the "God's Word" section of this meditation. See yourself as the various persons in the story: Jesus, the accused woman, one of the accusers. Have you ever acted like Jesus did in this passage? Have you ever been like a member of the hostile crowd? Has the accused woman's role ever been yours? Envision some practical applications of this meditation.

God's Word

The scribes and Pharisees brought a woman along who had been caught committing adultery; and making her stand there in the middle they said to Jesus, "Master, this woman was caught in the very act of committing adultery, and in the Law Moses has ordered us to stone women of this kind. What have you got to say?" They asked him this as a test, looking for an accusation to use against him. But Jesus bent down and started writing on the ground with his finger. As they persisted with their question, he straightened up and said, "Let the one among you who is guiltless be the first to throw a stone at her." Then he bent down and continued writing on the ground. When they heard this they went away one by one, beginning with the eldest, until the last one had gone and Jesus was left alone with the woman, who remained in the middle. Jesus again straightened up and said, "Woman, where are they? Has no one condemned you?" "No one, sir," she replied. "Neither do I condemn you," said Jesus. "Go away, and from this moment sin no more." (John 8:3–11)

Closing prayer:

Listen to me, O God, and answer me,
because I am poor and afflicted.
Yahweh, you are good and forgiving,
full of faithful love for all who pray to you.
Turn to me and have mercy on me;
strengthen me and save me.

(Psalm 86:1,5,16)

Charity

Theme: Love stands at the heart of Christian life. Dominic preached the Gospel of love and provided an example of gracious charity.

Opening prayer: Creator God, you are love, and I have heard your great commandment to love. Help me to grow in love of you so that I can more fully love my sisters and brothers with whom I travel this earthly pilgrimage.

About Dominic

Dominic's prayer and preaching revolved around these words from Matthew's Gospel:

> "You must love the Lord your God with all your heart, with all your soul, and with all your mind. This is the greatest and the first commandment. The second resembles it: You must love your neighbour as yourself." (Matthew 22:37–39)

Love means to seek and then foster the good of others in the context of their concrete situation. For Dominic, charity sometimes took the form of sharing what he had; and he commonly demonstrated his charity by preaching. Dominic knew that following in Jesus' footsteps was the way to peace, justice, and love. By urging his sisters and brothers to follow Jesus, he fostered their good: Jesus is the Way, the Truth, and the Life.

Biographers record that even when Dominic corrected or confronted his friars, he did so with charity. This account is found in Dominican sources:

> "He was happy, kind, patient, cheerful, compassionate and a comforter of the brethren. If he saw any of the brethren offending in any point, he walked past as if he had not seen it, but later, looking perfectly calm, he would address him with soothing words and say to him, 'Brother, you have done wrong; do penance.' In this kind way he led them all to do penance and make amends." (Tugwell, *Early Dominicans*, p. 77)

Dominic understood that as superior he had a God-given responsibility to confront wrongdoing among the friars. However, he treated the offender with dignity and respect. By urging the friars to live more kindly, justly, and peacefully, he helped draw them to life according to Christ, a life filled with light and love.

Pause: The Gospel calls us to a life of charity. How aptly does the word *charity* describe your daily life?

Dominic's Words

Dominic avidly studied the Gospel of Matthew and the Epistles of Paul, but he also claimed a third text as a source of his inspiration. Once a priest questioned him about this third source of inspiration:

> A priest after hearing him preach right eloquently and talk most learnedly upon the sacred Scriptures, made bold to ask him what books he studied most. The man of God gave him this answer, that he studied more in the book of charity than in any other; and this choice of his was most wisely made, for it is indeed an all-instructive book. (Conway and Jarrett, *Lives of the Brethren*, pp. 56–57)

This commitment to charity endured to the very end of his life. On his deathbed, Dominic bequeathed this heritage to his disciples:

> "These are, beloved ones, the inheritances that I leave you as my sons, have charity among you; hold to humility; possess voluntary poverty." (Jarrett, *Life*, p. 166)

Reflection

God is the creator of all that exists. People honor the Creator by honoring, cherishing, and nourishing the Creator's handiwork.

True Christian charity embraces all of creation. Charity preaches the Gospel. Charity feeds hungry people and visits prisoners. Charity conserves the land for future generations. Charity protects children from abuse and nurtures their minds and bodies. Charity reconciles enemies. Charity gives equal pay for equal work. Charity confronts evil and calls for conversion.

Dominic is called holy because he preached charity and acted accordingly. The litmus test for living in harmony with God's will is our charitable actions to our friends, family, enemies, and creation.

✧ Think of several persons whom you love well. These people reflect a small portion of God's love for you. Thank God for each of these gifts.

✧ The Dominican Primitive Constitutions make this statement about Franciscans, who were known to observe absolute poverty and simplicity of life:

> Friars Minor are to be welcomed lovingly and cheerfully, just like our own . . . and they are to be looked after as generously and politely as the house can afford. (Tugwell, *Early Dominicans*, p. 468)

One way of showing charity is by being hospitable. How hospitable are you? Are there ways in which you could be more welcoming?

✧ Jesus said:

"I give you a new commandment:
love one another;
you must love one another
just as I have loved you.
It is by your love for one another,
that everyone will recognise you
as my disciples."

(John 13:34–35)

✦ Identify the needy people of today.
✦ Reflect on the ways in which you come to the aid of needy and desperate people.
✦ Are there other ways that the charity of Christ compels you to show your love to other people?
✦ Ask for Christ's guidance in framing your attempts to be vigilant to those in need.

✧ Make an *examen of consciousness*. Are there instances or patterns in which you fall short of Christ's standard of charity? Ask the Holy Spirit to help you grow as a person of Christ, a person who is more loving.

✧ Jesus urges his followers to love their enemies. This remains the ultimate challenge for Christians, and only God's grace makes it possible.

✦ Most of us look upon certain aspects of ourselves as enemies: for example, parts of our body, a compulsion, or some fear. Name some of these enemies within yourself. Then ask yourself, How can I love my personal enemies?
✦ Frequently, people we dislike, fear, or even hate actually represent some aspect of ourselves that we dislike, fear, or hate. For instance, if we regularly become annoyed at a manipulator, quite possibly we dislike the manipulator we see in us. Make a list of several people who often annoy you or people whom you dislike or fear. Then, next to each name, write your reflections on this question: What annoying, unlikable, or fearful aspect of myself do I see in this person? Converse with Jesus about how you can embrace not only the external but, as important, the internal enemy.

✧ Reflect on the portions of chapter 13 of Paul's First Letter to the Corinthians provided in the "God's Word" section of this meditation. Consider the ways in which you can claim this text as a description of yourself.

God's Word

Though I command languages both human and angelic—if I speak without love, I am no more than a gong booming or a cymbal clashing. And though I have the power of prophecy, to penetrate all mysteries and knowledge, and though I have all the faith necessary to move mountains—if I am without love, I am nothing. Though I should give away to the poor all that I possess, and even give up my body to be burned—if I am without love, it will do me no good whatever.

Love is always patient and kind; love is never jealous; love is not boastful or conceited, it is never rude and never seeks its own advantage, it does not take offence or store up grievances. Love does not rejoice at wrongdoing, but finds its joy in the truth. It is always ready to make allowances, to trust, to hope and to endure whatever comes.

Love never comes to an end. . . .

As it is, these remain: faith, hope and love, the three of them; and the greatest of them is love. (1 Corinthians 13:1–13)

Closing prayer: Source of All Life and Love, every person, place, and thing in my life is your gift to me. Help me to reverence these gifts. Help me to show my love for you by growing in my loving regard for those persons and those aspects of creation with which you have blessed me.

Perseverance

Theme: Although he faced numerous difficulties and frustrations, Dominic remained steadfast in preaching the Gospel. God would guide, protect, and inspire him. Dominic believed this and was not disappointed.

Opening prayer: Gracious God, you set before me the task of contributing to your Reign on earth, and you promise to support me as I address that task. Help me to persevere throughout my successes and disappointments as I try to do your will.

About Dominic

This account of Dominic's efforts to convert the Albigensians gives a clear picture of Dominic's perseverance and also his sense of humor:

> Dominic travelled indefatigably round the countryside, visiting villages, towns, and châteaux, and setting an example by his way of life, which was more austere than that of the *perfecti* themselves.
>
> He was not always kindly received; far from it. "The enemies of truth," wrote Jordanus of Saxony, "made mock of him, throwing mud and other disgusting stuff at

him, and hanging wisps of straw on him behind his back." Such treatment was not calculated to worry a mind as enthusiastic as Dominic's.

From the same source we learn the reply which the Saint made to those heretics who asked him: "What would you do if we seized you by force?" He told them: "I should beg you not to kill me at one blow, but to tear me limb from limb, that thus my martyrdom might be prolonged; I would like to be a mere limbless trunk. . . ."

The characteristically Spanish exaggeration of these remarks must have discouraged his adversaries. Even though they persisted in regarding Dominic as an envoy of the Devil, they were forced to realize that with such a madman they could do nothing. He went singing through villages where men and women pursued him with threats and jeerings; when he was exhausted he would sleep by the roadside. (Zoé Oldenbourg, *Massacre at Montségur: A History of the Albigensian Crusade,* trans. Peter Green, p. 93)

After a decade of patient perseverance, companions began to join Dominic. He believed that preaching was God's work, not his own, and would be accomplished according to God's own schedule. Trust in Providence enabled Dominic to place himself at God's disposal until the time came to complete the work begun in Dominic.

Pause: Ponder this: In times of trouble, disappointment, and failure, what sustains you?

Dominic's Words

Dominic persevered because of a deep faith in God's love that was nourished by prayer. In times of difficulty, he also felt supported by the counsel and help of other people whose wisdom he trusted.

For example, one foundation of the order flourished in Bologna. Diana d'Andaló, daughter of a wealthy family of the area, desired to enter the order and establish a contemplative community of nuns in Bologna. Before granting permission, Dominic sought advice.

St. Dominic gathered his brethren and asked them what they thought about building a house of nuns which would be called and which would be a part of the Order. The brethren answered as they thought fit, and then St. Dominic said to them, "I do not want to give you my decision today; I want to consult the Lord. I will tell you what I think tomorrow." In his usual way, he turned his attention to prayer.

The next day, when he had finished praying, he sat down with the brethren in Chapter and said, "It is absolutely necessary, brethren, that a house of nuns should be built, even if it means putting off for a time the work on our own house." (Tugwell, *Early Dominicans*, pp. 395–396)

The story does not end here. Diana's family vigorously opposed her plan. As a result, the first time she entered the convent, they removed her forcibly, seriously harming her. As wealthy people of influence, her family had the power to wreak untold havoc upon Dominic and his work.

Nonetheless, armed with the advice of the community and his understanding of God's will, Dominic persevered. Even though the community was not solidly established until after his death, Dominic's determination and perseverance to respond to God's will provided the necessary incentive to his followers to overcome obstacles.

Reflection

Dominic's life is an example for all people of faith who are faced with the demanding challenges of remaining faithful to a project, a task, or a relationship from the beginning to resolution. He persevered even though not all of his endeavors came to happy endings. For instance, only a small number of the Albigensians converted. Nevertheless, convinced that he was armed with God's will, Dominic found the strength and stamina to persevere. God provided the grace necessary to hope, believe, and love.

✧ Take a mental tour of your entire life. How has God been faithful to you throughout all the chapters, happy and sad, of your life? How is God's perseverance in your life an invitation for you to persevere in your role in other people's lives?

✧ List several deeply rooted beliefs or convictions that are your foundations in times of turmoil, fear, disruption, or doubt. Write a brief account of a time when each of these convictions has been a rock of salvation for you. Then thank God for giving you these beliefs.

✧ What is your most conspicuous virtue? If your friends were asked to name your most outstanding virtue, what would they say? Ponder how you have been able to persevere in this virtue throughout your life. Thank God for this dimension of holiness.

✧ Meditate on the scriptural selection provided in the "God's Word" section. Repeat lines that particularly speak to you. Ask God what you are supposed to learn from these lines.

God's Word

We are subjected to every kind of hardship, but never distressed; we see no way out but we never despair; we are pursued but never cut off; knocked down, but still have some life in us; always we carry with us in our body the death of Jesus so that the life of Jesus, too, may be visible in our body. Indeed, while we are still alive, we are continually being handed over to death, for the sake of Jesus. . . .

But as we have the same spirit of faith as is described in scripture—I believed and therefore I spoke—we, too, believe and therefore we, too, speak, realising that [the One] who raised up the Lord Jesus will raise us up with Jesus in our turn . . . and you as well. You see, everything is for your benefit, so that as grace spreads, so, to the glory of God, thanksgiving may also overflow among more and more people.

That is why we do not waver; indeed, though this outer human nature of ours may be falling into decay, at the same time our inner human nature is renewed day by day. (2 Corinthians 4:8–16)

Closing prayer: O faithful God, your goodness and love is an invitation to me to become like you—a source of goodness and love for other people. Grant me the guidance and strength to persevere in responding to your invitation in my life, so that I will grow in closer intimacy with you and with your beauteous creation.

V·ERIT·A·S

✧ For Further Reading ✧

Hinnebusch, William A. *The Dominicans: A Short History.* Dublin, Ireland: Dominican Publications, 1985.

Jarrett, Bede. *Life of St Dominic, 1170–1221.* Westminster, MD: Newman Bookshop, 1947.

Tugwell, Simon, ed. *Early Dominicans: Selected Writings.* New York: Paulist Press, 1982.

Acknowledgments (*continued*)

The excerpts on pages 15–16 and 18 are from *The Comedy of Dante Alighieri: Paradise*, translated by Dorothy L. Sayers and Barbara Reynolds (Baltimore: Penguin Books, 1962), pages 159–160. Copyright © 1962 by Anthony Fleming.

The excerpts on pages 18, 19, 20–21, 25, 35, 48, 60, 71, 77, 92, and 109 are from *Life of St Dominic, 1170–1221*, by Bede Jarrett (Westminster, MD: Newman Bookshop, 1947), respectively on pages 11, 14, 21–22, 166, 98, 99–100, 98, 107, 110–111, 90–91, and 166.

The excerpts on pages 28–29 and 91 are from *The Dominicans: A Short History*, by William A. Hinnebusch (Dublin, Ireland: Dominican Publications, 1985), respectively on pages 6 and 13. Copyright © 1985 by Dominican Publications. Used with permission.

The excerpts on pages 29–30, 54, 85–86, 103 (first excerpt), and 108 are from *Lives of the Brethren of the Order of Preachers: 1206–1259*, translated by Placid Conway, edited by Bede Jarrett (London: Blackfriars Publications, 1955), respectively on pages 49–50, 53–54, 47–48, 56, and 56–57. Used by permission of Burns & Oates.

The excerpts on pages 34, 49, and 52–53 are from the English translation of *The Roman Missal*, translated by the International Commission on English in the Liturgy, Inc. (ICEL) (New York: Catholic Book Publishing Company, 1985), respectively on pages 680, 453, and 365. Copyright © 1973 by ICEL. All rights reserved.

The excerpts on pages 36, 37, 49, 61, 64, 72–73, 85, 91, 96–97, 98, 108, 109, and 114 are from *Early Dominicans: Selected Writings*, edited by Simon Tugwell (New York: Paulist Press, 1982), respectively on pages 101, 466, 394, 102, 153, 98–99, 16, 95, 91, 457, 77, 468, and 395–396. Copyright © 1982 by the Missionary Society of St. Paul the Apostle in the State of New York. Used by permission of Paulist Press.

The excerpt on page 39 is from *God Day by Day: Following the Weekday Lectionary*, vol. 4, by Marcel Bastin, Ghislain Pinckers, and Michel Teheux, translated by David Smith (New York: Paulist Press, 1985), page 71. Copyright © 1985 by the Missionary Society of St. Paul the Apostle in the State of New York. Used with permission.

The excerpts on pages 41–42 are from *Saint Dominic and His Times*, by M.-H. Vicaire, translated by Kathleen Pond (Green Bay, WI: Alt Publishing Company, 1964), pages 28–30. Copyright © 1964 by Darton, Longman & Todd.

The first excerpt on page 43 is from *St. Dominic: Servant but Friend*, by M. Assumpta O'Hanlon (London: B. Herder Book Company, 1954), page 45. Copyright © 1954 by B. Herder Book Company.

The second excerpt on page 43 is from *The Dominicans*, by John-Baptist Reeves (New York: Macmillan Company, 1930), page 68. Copyright © 1930 by the Macmillan Company.

Titles in the Companions for the Journey Series

Praying with Julian of Norwich

Praying with Francis of Assisi

Praying with Catherine of Siena

Praying with John Baptist de La Salle

Praying with Teresa of Ávila

Praying with Hildegard of Bingen

Praying with Ignatius of Loyola

Praying with Thérèse of Lisieux

Praying with Elizabeth Seton

Praying with Dominic

Praying with John of the Cross   Available summer 1993

Order from your local religious bookstore or from

Saint Mary's Press
702 TERRACE HEIGHTS
WINONA MN 55987-1320
USA